SpringerBriefs in Archaeology

SpringerBriefs in Archaeolo

Series Editors:
Douglas Comer
Helaine Silverman
Willem Willems

For further volumes:
http://www.springer.com/series/10186

ical Heritage Management

A. José Farrujia de la Rosa

An Archaeology of the Margins

Colonialism, Amazighity and Heritage Management in the Canary Islands

 Springer

A. José Farrujia de la Rosa
Sociedad Española de Historia de la Arqueología
La Laguna, Tenerife (Canary Islands)
Spain

ISSN 1861-6623   ISSN 2192-4910 (electronic)
ISBN 978-1-4614-9395-2   ISBN 978-1-4614-9396-9 (eBook)
DOI 10.1007/978-1-4614-9396-9
Springer New York Dordrecht Heidelberg London

Library of Congress Control Number: 2013951521

© The Author(s) 2014
This work is subject to copyright. All rights are reserved by the Publisher, whether the whole or part of the material is concerned, specifically the rights of translation, reprinting, reuse of illustrations, recitation, broadcasting, reproduction on microfilms or in any other physical way, and transmission or information storage and retrieval, electronic adaptation, computer software, or by similar or dissimilar methodology now known or hereafter developed. Exempted from this legal reservation are brief excerpts in connection with reviews or scholarly analysis or material supplied specifically for the purpose of being entered and executed on a computer system, for exclusive use by the purchaser of the work. Duplication of this publication or parts thereof is permitted only under the provisions of the Copyright Law of the Publisher's location, in its current version, and permission for use must always be obtained from Springer. Permissions for use may be obtained through RightsLink at the Copyright Clearance Center. Violations are liable to prosecution under the respective Copyright Law.
The use of general descriptive names, registered names, trademarks, service marks, etc. in this publication does not imply, even in the absence of a specific statement, that such names are exempt from the relevant protective laws and regulations and therefore free for general use.
While the advice and information in this book are believed to be true and accurate at the date of publication, neither the authors nor the editors nor the publisher can accept any legal responsibility for any errors or omissions that may be made. The publisher makes no warranty, express or implied, with respect to the material contained herein.

Printed on acid-free paper

Springer is part of Springer Science+Business Media (www.springer.com)

To Isabel, Otto, and Ana,
my particular polar circle

To my family

Acknowledgments

This book is the direct result of research carried out over the past four years. During this time I have had the opportunity to take part in various national and international conferences, and work abroad, and both experiences have helped to enrich the contents of this monograph through discussions held with other archaeologists and historians. I would therefore like to thank the following colleagues for sharing their ideas with me, because their comments have, without doubt, enhanced the perspective and depth of the work. First of all, I would like to thank Alain Schnapp, Professor of Classical Archaeology at the University of Paris 1 (Panthéon Sorbonne), former Director General of the Institut National d'Histoire de l'Art (INHA), and a leading world specialist in the history of archaeology. His examination of the history of Canarian archaeology has helped open up new perspectives that are crucial to understanding archaeological heritage management in the Canary Islands since the mid-nineteenth century in comparison with the European and international context. I also offer my most sincere thanks to Gonzalo Ruiz Zapatero, Professor of Prehistory at the Universidad Complutense de Madrid, and Tracy Ireland, Senior Lecturer in Cultural Heritage at the University of Canberra (Australia). Their comments have been particularly helpful in placing the case of the Canary Islands within an international context and in exploring the problematic of colonialism and postcolonialism in archaeological practice. My thanks are also due to Margarita Díaz-Andreu, an ICREA Research Professor in the Department of Prehistory at the University of Barcelona. Her knowledge of Spanish archaeology during the Franco regime and the effects of colonialism on archaeology and the management of culture and heritage in relation to tourism have, to a great extent, been a model for my approach to the case of the Canary Islands. Also, my gratitude to Bruce Maddy Weitzman, Principal Research Fellow at the Moshe Dayan Center for Middle Eastern and African Studies at Tel Aviv University, for sharing with me his knowledge of the Amazigh issue in North Africa.

I am also grateful to Helaine Silvermann, Professor of Anthropology, Latin American and Caribbean Studies, LAS Global Studies, and Member of the Center for East Asian and Pacific Studies at the University of Illinois, Urbana-Champaign. This book would not have been possible without her special interest in indigenous archaeology and the case of the Canary Islands, based on the *First International Conference on*

Best Practices in World Heritage Archaeology, in Menorca in April 2012. The exchange of ideas with Fernando Estévez González, Professor of Social Anthropology at the Universidad of La Laguna, has also been very valuable. I would like to thank him for reading the first draft of this book and for his comments, which have helped me to refine certain ideas and approaches, particularly those pertaining to tourism and postcolonialism. I would also like to thank Tarek Ode for the photographs that accompany this volume and which, without question, provide an opportunity for understanding a great many of the specific features of Canarian archaeology.

Contents

Chapter 1
Introduction

1.1 Introduction

This book analyzes the problematic of archaeological heritage management in the Canary Islands (Spain), an archipelago whose archaeology reveals significant features and differences in relation to the rest of Spain and, to an even greater extent, other European countries, inasmuch as it is essentially defined by its African roots. However, at the same time, Canarian archaeology also shares some of the most common characteristics of social histories of archaeology worldwide (including Europe). With regard to heritage management, Canarian archaeology belongs to the era of globalization, in which Western ideology has controlled the archaeological heritage management agenda by analyzing and interpreting heritage in terms of a Western cultural viewpoint (Ireland 2010). From this perspective, archaeology is fundamental to cultural identity and nation building because it helps in creating a cultural heritage or, in other words, the combination of tangible objects (sites, landscapes, structures, and artifacts) and intangible values (the ideas, customs, and knowledge that give rise to them) that archaeologists study. Archaeological heritage, therefore, has also been involved in perpetuating certain aspects of the historical master narratives of Europe, as is the case in the Canarian context.

Globalization, albeit in an earlier technological form, can be interpreted as the key process that has shaped the colonial world: exploration, imperialism, colonization, mass migration, and the spread of capitalism are processes crucially interwoven into the subsequent rise and spread of postcolonial nationalisms (Lydon and Rizvi 2010). Although in many nations globalization appears to have resulted in an intensification of the level and importance of nationalistic imagery, it is also clear that concepts of personal and collective identity, and therefore shared or social memory, have changed and fragmented in recent decades and that this should perhaps be understood as a cultural effect of globalization. Within these parameters, heritage can be seen not only as a global discourse, but also as a discourse of globalization through its promotion of the idea of heritage as material and authentic. Heritage thus occupies a dual position, as both a cause and effect of cultural globalization (Willems 2012).

Within this panorama, politics is understood here as the representation of interests and social identities. Therefore, in referring to the political use of archaeology and

A. J. Farrujia de la Rosa, *An archaeology of the margins*,
SpringerBriefs in Archaeology, DOI 10.1007/978-1-4614-9396-9_1,
© The Author(s) 2014

Fig. 1.1 Location of the
Canary Islands

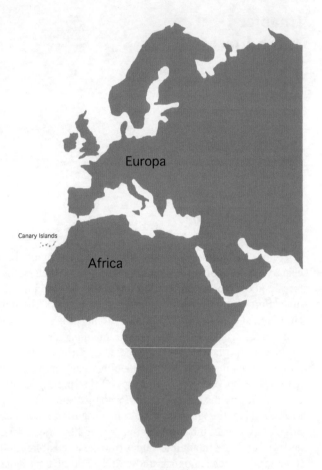

archaeological discourse, when analyzing the heritage management in the Canary
Islands, we are referring to social control and the imposition of the ideology deployed
by the discursive practice in question. In other words, political power is exercised by
means of this discourse and by excluding other discourses, whereas certain discursive
practices persist because they help to establish positions of power, status, and social
control (Foucault 2002, p. 14). History, in this sense, is an expression of identity
and its role has therefore always been subordinate to power; social, political, and
religious ideologies; and its knowledge has been linked to the ruling elite, the nation,
and the state. Because it is not a neutral form of knowledge, it is difficult for it to
become theoretical knowledge. The manipulation of history ultimately begins with
its own management of memory or oblivion, inasmuch as memory is projected with
a focus on particular themes, figures, and periods (Fig. 1.1).

In the case of the Canarian archipelago, its specific location close to the north-
western African coast has influenced its archaeological history and the present-day
archaeological heritage management, given that the Canary Islands are located on
the margins of Europe, belong to Spain, and therefore to the European Union, but in

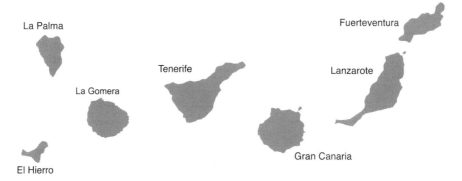

Fig. 1.2 The Canary Islands

geographical terms are part of Africa.[1] Moreover, the indigenous period that predates the European conquest of the islands during the fourteenth and fifteenth centuries is clearly African, or Amazigh (pl. Imazighen), in origin, and archaeological links can be established between the first inhabitants of the archipelago and the Morocco Atlas area, Tunisia, Algeria, and Libya (Fig. 1.2)[2].

The development of a European imperialist archaeology in the Canarian archipelago by foreign researchers, from the second half of the nineteenth century until well into the twentieth century was directly related to the colonial partitioning of Africa after 1880. Due to its geostrategic location in relation to the neighboring continent and to expansion throughout the South Atlantic region, the Archipelago became a "key" piece in the imperialist politics of countries such as France and Germany, eventually ensuring the involvement of French and German academics in archaeological studies of Canarian prehistory.

It is notable that a European power such as Great Britain, with clear colonial interests in North Africa, did not develop an imperialist archaeology in the Canary Islands. However, this was due to a very specific situation: the British sphere of influence in Africa was based essentially in the Eastern Mediterranean, to be more

---

[1] The Canary Islands form an archipelago of volcanic origins consisting of seven major islands situated northwest of the African continent on a level with the Sahara desert. The island closest to Africa (Lanzarote) lies approximately 100 km from its shores, and the farthest (Hierro) is 500 km away. The islands have a total area of 7,800 km². In administrative terms, they are divided into two provinces: Las Palmas de Gran Canaria (which includes the islands of Gran Canaria. Fuerteventura, and Lanzarote) and Santa Cruz de Tenerife (which includes Tenerife, La Palma, La Gomera, and El Hierro).

[2] The word *Amazigh* is the name chosen by the Berbers to refer to themselves. It signifies "nobility" and "magnanimity" and its use has been documented since the time of Ramses III (in the thirtieth century BC). There is also evidence of variations used as ethnonyms in ancient times and in the present day, which differ according to the period and source in question, as Chafik (2005, p. 14) and Tilmatine (2008, p. 36) have noted. Since the mid-nineteenth century, researchers have used the ethnonym *Guanche* to refer to the indigenous Canarian societies, although this is nowadays restricted to the ancient Tenerife populations (Farrujia 2005).

precise in the Upper Nile region. In any case, this did not prevent the British from maintaining an interest in the islands, in the form of pseudo-colonial trade relations with the Canary Islands: in terms of the import trade at the time, the result of developments in tourism that had stimulated imports of all types of materials and supplies needed for the hotels and sanatoriums that were being built, the Canaries basically imported cotton cloth, coal, and comestibles (biscuits, oil, and grain). The Canaries became another theater for the intense British–German commercial rivalry that had extended across the entire world, acquiring special notoriety in the colonial territories (Farrujia 2005).

Later, during the Franco dictatorship (1939–1975), the national unity of the whole Spanish state (including the Canary Islands) and the African aspirations of the regime clearly forced archaeology, once again, to be used outside academic circles to validate nationalist and colonialist aspirations. The non-Hispanic nature of the archaeological remains found in the Canary Islands, was simply ignored, if not given a different interpretation (Farrujia 2003).

Despite its unquestionable North African Imazighen roots, the archaeological studies pursued in the Canary Islands since the nineteenth century and during the Franco dictatorship always focused on the supposed European origins of the indigenous Canarians and their links to the major European cultures, therefore establishing the Canary Islands as part of universal history. Influenced by the political situation in the archipelago and the archaeological trends in vogue at the time, namely evolutionist theories followed by cultural historicism around 1939 and onwards, this played a disproportionate role in defining the image and identity of the indigenous Canarian societies and the consequent management of their heritage. The halls of the first scientific societies and the first museums echoed with speeches clearly advocating a European interpretation of the indigenous societies. Over time, this ethnocentric legacy has tainted archaeological heritage management up to the present day. Several clear examples of this are cited in this book, in analyzing the cases of the city of San Cristóbal de La Laguna on the island of Tenerife, the Tindaya Mountain in Fuerteventura, the Archaeological Parks of Belmaco and La Zarza and La Zarcita in La Palma, the Archaeological Park of El Julan in El Hierro, and, to a lesser extent, the Museum and Archaeological Park of Cueva Pintada de Gáldar in Gran Canaria.

From a theoretical perspective, this book therefore analyzes aspects such as the effects of colonialism and ethnocentrism on archaeological heritage management. It also examines the evolutionist and cultural–historical models used to analyze past societies and, ultimately, to create identities and influence archaeological heritage management itself.

From a practical point of view, the book presents a proposal for enhancing the archaeological heritage of the Canary Islands through the creation of archaeological parks (providing some concrete examples in the case of the city of La Laguna) and the active involvement of the local community, involving various proposals that are also detailed. Parallel to this, it considers the Canarian archipelago as part of a problematic that is not unique to this area but is an example of poor indigenous heritage management. The book therefore analyzes a Canary Islands heritage problem that is echoed in other parts of the world where the indigenous heritage is underrepresented.

Fig. 1.3 Indigenous people in La Gomera, from an illustration by Leonardo Torriani (1592)

In addition, it shows how the course of history and the politics of the past still have an excessive influence on the way in which the present-day archaeological heritage is interpreted and managed.

Prior to this, it is necessary to describe—although in a very schematic way—the archaeological situation in the Canary Islands, namely the types of sites, chronologies, material culture, and relationship to the North African Amazigh (Fig. 1.3).

1.2   The Great Dilemma: European Ancestors or Insular Imazighen?

The Imazighen from North Africa settled in the Canarian archipelago in the middle of the first millennium BC and developed a culture on the islands that can be linked to native North African societies and magical–religious practices associated with the religions of the ancient Amazigh.

The indigenous Canarians lived mainly in natural caves (and to a lesser extent in manmade caves cut into rocks), usually near the coast, 300–500 m above sea level. These caves were sometimes isolated but more commonly formed settlements, with burial caves nearby. Gran Canaria is the only island where settlements with stone houses forming important urban concentrations can be found, although isolated houses have also been documented. In terms of subsistence, animal husbandry was the main means of support for the indigenous societies in the different islands, with the exception of Gran Canaria where agriculture was more developed, including both dry and irrigated farming. The herds basically consisted of goats and sheep and, to

Fig. 1.4 Houses in an indigenous settlement in Barranco de los Gatos (Mogán, Gran Canaria). Photograph: Tarek Ode

a lesser extent, pigs, all of them imported from West North Africa and adequately adapted to the climate and environment. Gathering plants and fishing also provided significant food resources (Figs. 1.4 and 1.5).

Ceramics are the artifacts most commonly found in archaeological excavations and also the most widely studied. This is due to the research possibilities they offer, using a cultural–historical approach (which still prevails among Canarian archaeologists), for establishing timelines, food consumption patterns, stylistic trends, and so on. In the Canary Islands they are typically varied, with each island presenting both formal and decorative differences. The only common feature is that they were coil-built instead of using a wheel. Ceramic items were often incised or burnished, in particular in Gran Canaria, where painted decorations in shades of red, black, and white were also common. The La Palma ceramics provide the best stratigraphic sequence, in four phases, although the Gran Canaria ceramics are undoubtedly the most complex, due to the variety of shapes, handles, and decorative features. Gran Canaria ceramics also exhibit the clearest affinities with North African Amazigh ceramics. The Tenerife vessel forms enable parallels to be drawn with those documented in Mauritania and in the central and southern Sahara regions (Farrujia 2004) (Fig. 1.6).

The raw materials used in the lithic industry were obsidian and basalt, and the most common tools were burins, borers, racloirs, and scrapers. Typical polished stone items were ground stones, used to grind cereals. In terms of the bone industry, which was based mainly on ovicaprine bones, grainers and awls for use in leatherwork were common, as well as fish hooks. Antlers were also used to make tools for ploughing or

Fig. 1.5 Houses in an indigenous settlement in Barranco de los Gatos (Mogán, Gran Canaria). Detail. Photograph: Tarek Ode

Fig. 1.6 Indigenous ceramics from Tenerife (*Gánigo*). Photograph: Museo Arqueológico de Tenerife

Fig. 1.7 Indigenous ceramics
from Gran Canaria.
Photograph: El Museo
Canario

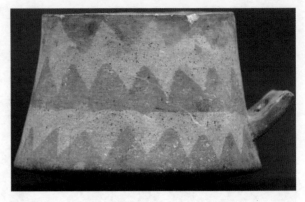

were set in wood to be used as projectiles (spears). There was also an important wood
industry, primarily represented by shepherd's crooks, combs, shields, containers, and
doors for manmade caves and houses (Fig. 1.7).

The majority of the plant fibers used by the indigenous Canarians for clothing and
basket-making came from the round-head bulrush (*Holoschoenus vulgaris*), which
was used to make mats, baskets, bags, and shrouds, as well as garments, which were
also manufactured from goatskin (Arco 1993).

In terms of social and political organization, there was a system of matrilineal
descent in most of the islands, in which inheritance was passed on via the female line.
Social status and wealth were hereditary and determined the individual's position in
the social pyramid, which consisted of the king (known as the *Guanarteme* in Gran
Canaria and *Mencey* in Tenerife), the relatives of the king, the lower "nobility,"
villeins, plebeians, and, finally, executioners, butchers, embalmers, and prisoners.

With regard to faith, the indigenous Canarians, like the North African Imazighen
groups, worshipped two celestial divinities, the sun and the moon, and sacred natural
places such as particular mountains, rocks, and caves. Their religion revolved around
the need for rainwater, on which the pasture land and crops, and therefore the food
for the indigenous people and their livestock, depended. Religious offices were
usually held by men, although in Gran Canaria and Fuerteventura these duties were
performed by women. Some indigenous sites have been associated with this cult,
such as the cave paintings in Gran Canaria whose interiors display painted geometric
motifs, the cup and groove sites, consisting of small spherical depressions carved into
the rock and linked by manmade channels related to the spilling of libations, and the
sacrificial altars, built in stone and varying in shape although mainly circular, used
to burn animals sacrificed as offerings to the gods (Mederos and Escribano 2002).

The world of death was also related to cultural practices. In the Canary Islands,
burial sites are one of the most common finds, although they have been plundered
continuously since the eighteenth century. The indigenous Canarians believed that
life continued in another form after death and therefore supplied the corpse with
provisions (ceramics, food, awls, beads, rush bags, etc.). They laid the bodies to rest
by placing them on beds of stone, vegetation, animal skins, and the like to avoid

Fig. 1.8 Indigenous mummy
in the Tenerife Archaeological
Museum. Photograph: Museo
Arqueológico de Tenerife

physical contact with the earth. The most common method of laying out corpses was
to place them supine inside natural caves or shelters. In Gran Canaria they were also
placed in excavated caves or tombs (Arco et al. 1992).

Indigenous funeral rituals also included mummification, which was reserved for
members of the "nobility" (as a prestige practice) and has been documented primarily
in Tenerife and Gran Canaria (Farrujia 2004; Fig. 1.8).

Further evidence of the North African origins of the indigenous Canary Island
populations can be seen in the rock engravings, featuring a script classified as
Libyan-Berber that shows clear affinities with scripts recorded in Libya and Algeria. Moreover, from a genetic point of view, the closest counterparts to 55% of the
descendants of the indigenous populations are found in the Maghreb.[3]

Regarding the early colonization of the islands, we are still far from being able
to form a final opinion regarding the situation for the Archipelago as a whole, because the extent of research varies widely from island to island.[4] Nevertheless, an
examination of the Lybico-Berber inscriptions and radiocarbon dates available from
some sites on the islands indicate that the Canary Islands can be divided into two
geographically overlapping areas of Amazigh influence in different times:

a. An archaic Amazigh culture in the sixth century BC, including El Hierro, Tenerife,
   Gran Canaria, La Palma, and La Gomera
b. A Romanized Amazigh culture dating from the time of Augustus and Juba II, including Lanzarote, Fuerteventura, Gran Canaria, El Hierro, and Tenerife (Farrujia
   et al. 2010)[5]

On the basis of current research, it is possible to refer to the existence of relations between some islands during the indigenous period (Tenerife-La Gomera, or

[3] Autochthonous (E-M81) and prominent (E-M78 and J-M267) Amazigh Y-chromosome lineages
were detected in Canarian indigenous remains, confirming the northwest African origins of their
ancestors, thus validating previous mitochondrial DNA results (Fregel et al. 2009).

[4] The present-day situation is unpromising because, although research in recent decades has con-
solidated the Canarian–African relationship, it is clear that there is still no consensus in terms of
origins. (How did the islands become populated and colonized? How did the first settlers arrive?)
In addition, isolated radiocarbon dates obtained recently, which are not representative of the entire
archipelago (e.g., those from the Buenavista site in Lanzarote, which produce a date of C-14 for
the 10th century BC), suggest an earlier occupation of the archipelago (Atoche 2011), specifically
in the case of Lanzarote, which is closest to the African coast.

[5] In the islands of Lanzarote and Fuerteventura, Latin-Canarian inscriptions have been documented
near the Lybico-Berber inscriptions, which enable reference to be made to the presence on these
islands of a Romanized Amazigh culture, which may have extended to El Hierro, Tenerife, and
Gran Canaria as well.

Fig. 1.9 Lybico-Berber
inscription, La Caleta (El
Hierro). Photograph: Tarek
Ode

Lanzarote-Fuerteventura-Gran Canaria), inasmuch as certain aspects of the material culture would appear to indicate this. However, some cultural features in certain islands are not found in others. Although they share the same base, the indigenous island cultures developed in isolation, with very little contact with the exterior. Given this, the poor quality of the ceramics, except in the case of Gran Canaria, leads to the conclusion that later inter-island and even cross-cultural exchanges were rare, indicating cultural isolation until the time when the islands were conquered by the Europeans in the fourteenth century (Fig. 1.9)[6].

The entire indigenous culture, which had existed in the Canary Islands since the middle of the first millennium BC, began to disappear irreversibly following the conquest and colonization of the archipelago that began in the Late Middle Ages.

It should be noted that the indigenous Canarian culture can only be explained by a continental-Africana ethnogenesis which is inseparable from the culture of certain ethnic Amazigh groups who lived approximately 2,000 years ago. The culture developed in the Canarian archipelago by Imazighen societies was clearly influenced by insular isolation and adaptation to the island environment under conditions which meant that they were virtually cut off from contact with the African continent and

---

[6] For a more extensive and detailed perspective on the archaeology of the Canary Islands, see the works of Tejera and González (1987); Arco et al. (1992); Arco (1993); Tejera (2001); Mederos and Escribano (2002); and Farrujia (2004).

Fig. 1.10 The Ifara rock art site (Granadilla, Tenerife). Photograph: Tarek Ode

other ethnic Amazigh groups. This has made the indigenous archaeology of the Canary Islands an extraordinary, marginal and almost unclassifiable historical example of Amazigh or (North) African culture. In other words, the indigenous Canarian universe was unarguably Amazigh, although from the point of view of "positive culture" it is a unique case and an extraordinary product of involution (due to isolation) and adaptation to an island environment. The archaeological evidence (ceramics, rock inscriptions, etc.) and anthropological/genetic type (DNA) evidence are indisputable. However, there are many gaps in our understanding of the circumstances in which the first settlers arrived in the Canary Islands. We still do not know how or why the North African Amazigh landed in the Canary Islands in the middle of the first millennium BC, although the early colonization of the islands has recently been related to Phoenician–Punic influence in the Atlantic: the islands could have been colonized by Phoenician traders who brought over North Africans (Figs. 1.10, 1.11 and 1.12).[7]

---

[7] See the work of González Antón and Arco Aguilar (2007) or Atoche (2011), among others.

Fig. 1.11 The Lomo de
Marrera rock art site (Güímar,
Tenerife). The checkered
motifs documented in the
Canary Islands have clear
affinities with those found in
the Upper Atlas region of
Morocco. Photograph: Tarek
Ode

Fig. 1.12 The Lomo de
Marrera rock art site (Güímar,
Tenerife). Photograph: Tarek
Ode

1.3 The Gradual Disappearance of the Indigenous Canarian Heritage

The Canary Islands were rediscovered in the Middle Ages as a result of European
expansion in the Atlantic, a process initiated by Portugal, Aragon, and Italy in the
fourteenth century, and later joined by Castile in the fifteenth century.[8] This process
was neither quick nor continuous and lasted for almost the entire century. From
1402 until 1477, the conquest was led by the nobility and carried out by the Norman
French, affecting the islands of Lanzarote (1402), Fuerteventura, La Gomera, and

---

[8] Obviously, at that time the term "European" did not have the same connotations as it has nowadays.
In using it, following Stevens (1997, p. 86), I am referring to a concept of Europe which is
synonymous with Christendom. It is, therefore, a term used with cultural connotations rather than
geographical implications and describes a homogeneous world in which people believed in one sole
religion and were all governed by the same laws and moral criteria. The opposite term, "Islam,"
designated the religion of the great majority of the inhabitants of Africa and the Mediterranean
region of Asia.

El Hierro (1405). This phase marked the beginning of the true occupation of the islands, establishing effective control over the territory and the imposition of an administrative–fiscal system. However, this conquest by the nobility was marked by a slowness in establishing new settlements, due to the unprofitability of the venture and the unattractiveness of the feudal system in the eyes of the settlers.

From 1478 onwards, the crown, headed by the Catholic kings, played a larger part in the conquest, and the regal phase began. This new stage led to the annexation of Gran Canaria (1483), La Palma (1493), and Tenerife (1496) by the Kingdom of Castile. Once all the islands had been conquered, the final result was a political map divided into two territories, the regal and the seigniorial, and this division remained throughout the *Ancien Régime*, disappearing only when the seigniorial or manorial regime ended in the nineteenth century.

Within an international context, the fifteenth and sixteenth centuries also marked the beginning of the exploration and colonization of large parts of the world by western European countries. Sailors began to make contact with indigenous hunter-gatherers and farmers in the Americas, Africa, and the Pacific, as well as the indigenous Canarians. Descriptions of these people and their customs began to circulate throughout Europe, and their tools and clothing, brought back by travelers, were displayed as curiosities. At first, the discovery of groups of humans who had no knowledge of metalwork and whose customs were totally different from Christian teachings seemed to confirm the traditional medieval view that the groups originating farther away from the Near East, the cradle of humanity, were the farthest removed from divine revelation and therefore more morally and technologically backward (Trigger 2006, p. 61; Farrujia 2004, Chap. 2).

As a result of the rediscovery, conquest, and colonization of the Canary Islands, a series of ethnohistorical written sources emerged (consisting of chronicles, reports, memoirs, and general early histories) that focused on the islands. These sources, written by European authors rather than indigenous Canarians, typically included chapters or sections devoted to the indigenous population of the archipelago, observed from a perspective that was clearly conditioned by a Judeo-Christian world view and classical tradition (Farrujia 2004; Baucells 2004). This explains why most of the information about the indigenous world was clearly influenced by "western thought" and, to a lesser extent, by direct observation. The other stumbling block was that the West had never attempted to listen to the Other, the indigenous people, but had always assimilated them into its own culture, both before and after Christianity, meaning that there was no tradition in Western culture of endeavoring to understand and respect the Other, or the foreigner. This explains the difficulties that ensued for the Spanish (and Europeans in general) in understanding the culture of the Canary Islands or, in a later but parallel context, the Amerindians, as well as the hesitations and doubts that sometimes even affected the same individual concerning the nature of the indigenous peoples and their place within a human and international context, as people and as individuals living in organized societies.

With the passing of time, the legacy of the individual communities that inhabited the different islands in the archipelago up to the time of the European colonization—and provided evidence of their way of life and adaptation and survival strategies in this island environment—began to disappear irreversibly as a direct result of the gradual disappearance of the indigenous Canarian societies. In the case of the Canary Islands, unlike the situation on the American continent (Pérez 2006) or in Australia (Veracini 2006), there is no historical continuity between the indigenous, precolonial, and postcolonial societies, because the conquest and subsequent colonization of the Canary Islands by the Crown of Castile led to the gradual physical destruction of almost the entire indigenous society.[9] This is why in the Canary Islands there is no indigenous archaeology, that is, archaeological research and heritage management produced by and for indigenous people. In fact, the Canarian economy became characterized essentially by a model based on agricultural development, which, in turn, formed part of the Atlantic and international economy. This led to the development of a dependent and peripheral economy on the islands from the beginning of the sixteenth century. The resulting colonial society was composed of a ruling group (the aristocracy, clergy, and merchants, i.e., those who held political positions and controlled the economy) and the majority whom they ruled (laborers, those marginalized for religious reasons, and slaves, including the indigenous Canarians).

In the case of the Canary Islands therefore, the concept of "indigenous" implies clear temporal connotations: it refers to the populations present on the islands since the time of the first settlements in the archipelago (in the middle of the first millennium BC) until its rediscovery in the sixteenth century by Europeans.[10]

At the end of the seventeenth century, as a consequence of the gradual disappearance of the indigenous Canarian people and their culture, their legacy began to be viewed from a more archaeological than ethnohistorical perspective. In this sense, as Gómez Escudero himself stated at the end of this century, in Gran Canaria, "Now in these islands houses and (native) tombs have been discovered, made of fine wood" (1993, p. 103). As has been argued elsewhere (Farrujia 2010), it was not until the end of the seventeenth century that the ethnohistorical approach gave way to an archaeological approach. Earlier, in the fifteenth century, the indigenous Canarian populations were still thriving and, because they were not fossils, were not considered from a prescientific archaeological perspective. It was not until the mid-eighteenth century that antiquarian studies began in the Canary Islands.

The rediscovery of the Canary Islands by the Europeans therefore led to the gradual disappearance of the indigenous settlements, the elimination of material items from the indigenous culture, the appropriation of indigenous areas (which were occupied by the new settlers and by the emerging colonial society), and the imposition of ways of life and systems of social organization and production governed by a Western-European world view, values and regulatory mechanisms that were

---

[9] Indigenous female lineages have survived in present-day populations since the conquest, experiencing only a moderate decline, whereas indigenous male lineages have fallen consistently and have been replaced by European lineages (Fregel et al. 2009).

[10] In North America indigenous people may be called by general names such as "American Indians," "Native Americans," "Native Alaskan corporations," or "Native Hawaiians." In Canada they may be referred to as "First Nations" or "Meti," in Australia "Aboriginals," in New Zealand, "Maori," and in Scandinavia "Sami." In the Canary Islands, they can be called indigenous Canarian people or insular Imazighen.

alien to the indigenous Canarian world. Over time, the arrival in the archipelago of an imperialist archaeology, developed during the nineteenth century and a good part of the twentieth century, would help perpetuate this Western, European interpretation of the indigenous Canarian past.

1.4 The North African Imazighen

The scenario described above clearly contrasts with the North African context, in which the Imazighen, the indigenous populations of the area, have maintained a constant presence since ancient times. This African region has experienced various forms of colonization which, through contacts established with the indigenous people, have given the area a special character. North Africa has been the focus of interactions with "late-comers," from the founding of Carthage in around 814 BC to the arrival of the French and Spanish colonizers in the twentieth century. The Amazigh-speaking peoples of ancient times, having already encountered the Phoenicians in Carthage, then came into contact with the original "globalizer" (Rome), later resulting in Byzantium. This was followed, more profoundly, by Islam, with the Muslim presence, starting in around 647 AD, proving the most significant (El-Aissati 2005).

By the seventeenth and eighteenth centuries, Arabic had come to predominate in Tunisia and Algeria, although in Morocco the majority of the population continued to live within Amazigh-speaking tribal frameworks. It was only in the nineteenth century that Europe returned to the Maghreb in full triumph, inaugurating another wave of integration within the world economic system through "imperialism" (Maddy-Weitzman 2006). After independence in Morocco (1956), Tunisia (1957), and Algeria (1962), the march against colonization was led from two different and conflicting fronts. The roundtable and discussion sessions involving "representatives" of national interests and the colonial administration were led by an urban, mostly non-Berber elite, whereas the fighting on the ground and armed resistance was more the business of the Berbers (the Amazigh manifesto and other references) (Chafik 2005; Maddy-Weitzman 2012).

The call for the recognition of a distinct Berber identity has been gaining popularity, particularly following the independence of Morocco and Algeria. One of the first nongovernmental institutions to specialize in promoting Berber culture and language was the *Académie Berbère,* founded in Paris in 1967 by a group of Amazigh activists. The *Académie Berbère* was an eye-opener for many Berbers. Its main goal was to promote Berber culture and research Berber culture and civilization. The fact that it was founded outside Algeria was probably due to Algerian restrictions on nongovernmental and cultural organizations (which remained in force until the beginning of the 1990s). In the same year, *"L'Association Marocaine de la Recherche et de l'Echange Culturel* (The Moroccan Association for Research and Cultural Exchange)" was founded in Morocco, with similar goals to those of the *Académie Berbère* (Ramos 2012).

The creation in 1990 of two departments for the study of the Berber language and culture in Algeria has certainly opened more doors for students interested in this field. The universities of Tizi Ouzou (since 1990) and Bejaia (since 1991) have been responsible for a number of students graduating in Berber language and literature.[11] The call for recognition of Berber cultural and linguistic rights was formalized in a document initially signed by six cultural associations in Agadir (Morocco) in 1991. This document, known as *la Charte d'Agadir*," is a protest against Berber marginalization and presents demands that include recognition of Berber as a national language in the Constitution, its standardization, and its inclusion in the school curriculum.[12]

The scope of the Berber movement was considerably enlarged by the founding in 1995 of the *"Congrès Mondial Amazigh* (CMA)," the World Amazigh Congress, a transnational nongovernmental institution that aims to defend and promote the cultural identity of the Berber nation and support its development in all domains, inside and outside the Tamazgha (North Africa, including the Canary Islands) and calls for official recognition of the Amazigh identity (Chafik 2005; El-Aissati 2005, p. 67).

The first meeting took place in Tafira (Gran Canaria, Canary Islands) on August 27th–30th, 1997 and showed that the Imazighen represent an important part of the present-day sociocultural reality of the Maghreb nation states and their language and culture are not merely relics of ancient times. The choice of the conference site was symbolic: the Canary Islands, better known as a place for general sun worship, were once inhabited by the Guanches, whose origins are Amazigh. In addition, the Canarian archipelago marks the westernmost point of Tamazgha. The Canary Islands were therefore intended to symbolize the process of deculturation by colonization opposed by the Imazighen, and also cultural resistance. Many North African Imazighen were rather surprised to learn about the commitment of their newly discovered Amazigh brothers from the Canary Islands. The fact that, even after having lost the language (Tamazight), they felt that they belonged to the wider Amazigh community, was once again considered unmistakable proof of the Imazighen resolve to keep their culture alive (Kratochwil 1999). However, this should be understood as the construction of an ethnic identity, as an *imagined community*, following Benedict Anderson's concept.[13] The most obvious expression of this newly rediscovered sense of belonging was the T-shirts worn by Canarians saying: "No soy europeo, soy bereber" (I am not European, I am Berber). Thus, a sense of togetherness was asserted, which astonished even the Amazigh people of North Africa. Skepticism emerged, however, as separatist slogans such as "Free Canarians" were displayed alongside the Amazigh motto. In a sense, Canarian demands for independence from

---

[11] *La charte d'Agadir* is available online (http://www.mondeberbere.eom/mouvement:charte.htm).

[12] See also http://www.congresmondial-amazigh.org/.

[13] An imagined community is different from an actual community because it is not (and, for practical reasons, cannot be) based on every face-to-face interaction between its members. A nation, therefore, is a socially constructed community, imagined by the people who perceive themselves as part of that group (Anderson 2006). Imagined communities can be seen as a form of social constructionism on a par with Edward Said's concept of imagined geographies (Said 1997).

Spain were voiced by taking advantage of the World Congress and the pan-Amazigh atmosphere, and by appealing to their Amazigh roots.[14]

Several conservative Canarian political parties protested against any claims for independence, inasmuch as the Amazigh World Congress had been declared to be of cultural interest, and was financed largely from public funds. Nevertheless, according to Kratochwil (1999) and Maddy-Weitzmann (2012, p. 136), it was impossible to ignore the political problems completely, especially those of the North African Member States.[15]

Another important achievement of the Amazigh movement took place more recently, in October 2001, when the first higher institute for Berber research was created in Rabat, Morocco, by royal decree, under the name of the *"Institut Royal de la Culture Amazighe (IRCAM)."* This institute is the only one in Morocco with an official mandate to carry out Berber research, produce school textbooks, and deal with issues related to Berber culture (Maddy-Weitzman 2012).

The current number of Imazighen, or speakers of one of the Amazigh language varieties,[16] has remained a matter of estimates: the figures suggest around 25% of the Algerian population (with the highest concentrations in mountainous areas such as Kabylia, the Aures mountains, and the Mzab), around 45% of the Moroccan population (with the highest concentrations in the Rif area, the Atlas Mountains, and the Sous Valley), 1% of the Tunisian population (mostly on the island of Djerba), a few thousand in Libya (mostly in Jbel Nefousa), and around one million in the southern part of Algeria and the northern parts of Mali and Niger, commonly known as the Tuaregs (El-Aissati 2005, p. 60).

It was during this phase, defined by international recognition of the Amazighity, that Ahmed Sabir's book (2008) was published, focusing on the linguistic and cultural links between the indigenous Canarians and the Imazighen from the area corresponding to present-day South Morocco (the Sus and Dra regions). The book was published

---

[14] The Canary Islands Independence Movement (CIIM), also known as the Movement for the Independence and Self-Determination of the Canaries Archipelago (MPAIAC, from Spanish Movimiento por la Autodeterminación e Independencia del Archipiélago Canario), is a defunct independentist organization that had a radio station in Algiers and resorted to violence in attempts to force the Spanish government to create an independent state in the Canary Islands. The Canary Islands Independence Movement was started by Antonio Cubillo (1930–2013) in 1964. Based in Algeria, the MPAIAC was recognized in 1968 by the Organization of African Unity. Its armed struggle was carried out by the group's armed wing, the Fuerzas Armadas Guanches (FAG), which in 1976 bombed a mall in Las Palmas de Gran Canaria. The CIIM or MPAIAC ceased activity after the Spanish government created the Autonomous Community of the Canarian Archipelago in 1982. The political wing of MPAIAC was known as Canarian Workers Party, Partido de los Trabajadores Canarios (PTC). It did not manage to rule any municipality in the islands before disbanding. The movement has recently undergone a modest renaissance, but only from the political wing (Gari 1992; Farrujia 2004).

[15] For example, most of the Algerian delegates were prevented from taking part in the conference at the very last moment, and the delegates from Libya ran the risk of being sanctioned by the Libyan state on their return.

[16] The major Amazigh language groups are Tarifit, Tamazight, and Tashelhit in Morocco (from north to south), Kabyle and the Choaui varieties in Algeria.

by the IRCAM, the institution responsible for politically monitoring the Amazigh question and for promoting studies and research in this area in Morocco.

1.5   Perspective and Thematic Structure of the Book

A rich and original indigenous archaeological heritage of North African origins remains in the Canary Islands which, unfortunately, has not been well preserved or managed in many cases. The main consequence of this is that many of these cultural assets are in a poor state of repair. Taking this problem into consideration, this book analyzes how the Canarian archaeological heritage has been managed, from the nineteenth century to the present day, and the current policies for the management, protection, and dissemination of this indigenous Canarian heritage.

In terms of content, the book is organized into three thematically related chapters covering different periods of time, from the nineteenth century to the present day. The first chapter briefly analyzes the origins of archaeological research in the Canary Islands (1868) and the development of the evolutionist theories that enabled the indigenous Canarian population to be linked to European, specifically French, prehistory. In addition, it pays particular attention to the archaeological heritage management that began to develop at the time in the Canaries, based on scientific societies and museums, which laid the foundations for a management model that remained until the outbreak of the Spanish Civil War in 1936.

The second chapter briefly analyzes the consequences of the Franco dictatorship (1939–1975) for research and heritage management in the Canary Islands, with reference to the centralization of management, controlled by the *Comisaría General de Excavaciones Arqueológicas* (General Commission for Archaeological Excavations) based in Madrid. It also reflects on how the Franco management model remained in force until well into the 1990s, resulting in a lack of understanding of the indigenous context and the persistence of cultural–historical models that supported the idea of links between the Guanches and Europe, in particular the relationship between the Guanches and the Iberian populations in the Iberian Peninsula.

The third chapter, which represents the central focus of the monograph, analyzes issues relating to the globalization of archaeological heritage management, the globalization of archaeology itself, the recovery of the elitist heritage, cultural diversity, and the protection of heritage and the collective memory, all recurring themes nowadays in the management of cultural assets. In terms of respecting the collective memory and local community, it is argued that the value of archaeological heritage assets is proportional to the importance the community ascribes to them and not how they are categorized by the public administration or specialists in the field. Parallel to this, consideration is given to the inadequate regional administration policies designed to enhance the local community's appreciation of the precolonial heritage of the Canary Islands, in order to enhance the value of the indigenous archaeological heritage in society. The case of Gran Canaria is exceptional, as it is one of the few

Canary islands with an integral heritage management policy that genuinely considers the indigenous past.

This chapter also analyzes the protection of the indigenous archaeological heritage, citing examples of different Archaeological Parks. In relation to this point, certain issues associated with tourism, conservation, and dissemination of the archaeological heritage are also analyzed.

Finally, the concluding chapter clearly summarizes the main ideas concerning the management of the archaeological heritage in the Canary Islands and how the management model needs to be significantly reformulated in order to introduce new heritage policies aimed at valuing the Amazigh legacy that predates the conquest.

In relation to the title of the book, the concept of an *archaeology of the margins* as applied to the case of the Canary Islands was coined by Professor Alain Schnapp in his prologue to my book *En busca del pasado guanche . Historia de la Arqueología en Canarias (1868–1968)*. The history of archaeology in the Canary Islands is precisely this, a history of a marginal area facing the harsh imperatives of a modernity desired by a distant centralizing state and colonial traditions that have endured for centuries. The archaeology of the Canary Islands is, as Schnapp points out, an important chapter in the history of archaeology, understood in terms of its relationship to societies, colonial strategies, and political ambitions. Canarian archaeology has changed, as has British and French archaeology and, during the lengthy Franco period, experienced a conservative authoritarian regime that for a long time kept its distance from more recent universal scientific discoveries. This monograph therefore examines the way in which scientific knowledge or understanding has been constructed, the nature of its a priori historical features and elements of positivism from which ideas have emerged (Foucault 2001, p. 7), and how this baggage has had repercussions for archaeological heritage management.

The book therefore aims to reflect the fact that the margins are as important as the centers, albeit in different ways, in terms of understanding the complex and unpredictable relationships between the past and the present. In this sense the research is, in the words of Marcel Mauss (1989), the study of a "total social fact."

References

Anderson, B. (2006). *Imagined Communities: Reflections on the origin and spread of Nationalism.* London: Verso.

Arco Aguilar, M. C. (1993). *Recursos vegetales en la Prehistoria de Canarias.* Santa Cruz de Tenerife: Cabildo Insular de Tenerife.

Arco Aguilar, M. C., Jiménez Gómez, M. C., & Navarro, M. (1992). *La arqueología en Canarias: del mito a la ciencia.* Santa Cruz de Tenerife (Spain): Interinsular. Ediciones Canarias.

Atoche Peña, P. (2011). Excavaciones arqueológicas en el sitio de Buenavista Lanzarote): nuevos datos para el estudio de la colonización protohistórica del archipiélago canario. *Gerión, 29*(1), 59–82.

Baucells Mesa, S. (2004). *Crónicas, Historias, Relaciones y otros relatos: las fuentes narrativas del proceso de interacción cultural entre aborígenes canarios y europeos (siglos XIV a XVII).* Las Palmas de Gran Canaria (Spain): Edición de la Fundación Caja Rural de Canarias.

Chafik, M. (2005). *Treinta y tres siglos de la Historia de los Imazighen (Bereberes)*. Rabat (Morocco): Institut Royal de la Culture Amazighe. Centre de la Traduction, de la Documentation de l'Edition et de la Communication.

El-Aissati, A. (2005). A socio-historical perspective on the Amazigh (Berber) cultural movement in North Africa. *Afrika Focus, 18*(1–2), 59–72.

Farrujia de la Rosa, A. J. (2003). The Canary Islands under Franco's dictatorship: Archaeology, national unity and African aspirations. *Journal of Iberian Archaeology, 5,* 209–222.

Farrujia de la Rosa, A. J. (2004). Ab Initio (1342–1969). *Análisis historiográfico y arqueológico del primitivo poblamiento de Canarias.* Col. Árbol de la Ciencia (Vol. 2). Sevilla: Artemisa Ediciones.

Farrujia de la Rosa, A. J. (2005). Imperialist archaeology in the Canary Islands. French and German studies on prehistoric colonization at the end of the 19th century. British Archaeological Reports. International Series, 1333. Oxford: Archaeopress.

Farrujia de la Rosa, A. J. (2010). *En busca del pasado guanche. Historia de la Arqueología en Canarias (1868–1968). Preface by Alain Schnapp.* Santa Cruz de Tenerife (Spain): Edicion Ka.

Farrujia de la Rosa, A. J., Pichler, W., Rodrigue, A., & García, M. (2010). The Lybico-Berber and Latino-Canarian Scripts and the colonization of the Canary Islands. *African Archaeological Review, 27*(1), 13–41.

Foucault, M. (2001 [1966]). *Las palabras y las cosas. Una arqueología de las ciencias humanas (Les mots et les choses. Une archéologie des sciences humaines).* Mexico: Siglo XXI Editores.

Foucault, M. (2002 [1970]). *El orden del discurso (L'ordre du discours).* Barcelona: Tusquets Editores.

Fregel, R., Gomes, V., Gusmão, L., González, A. M., Cabrera, V. M., Amorim, A. & Larruga, J. M. (2009). Demographic history of Canary Islands male gene pool: replacement of native lineage by European, BMC EvolutionaryBiology. http://www.biomedcentral.com/content/pdf/1471-2148-9-181.pdf. Accessed 2 Feb 2012.

Gari Hayek, D. (1992). *Historia del nacionalismo canario: historia de las ideas y de la estrategia política del nacionalismo canario en el siglo XX.* Santa Cruz de Tenerife (Spain): Editorial Benchomo.

Gómez Escudero, P. (1993). Libro Segundo prosigue la Conquista de Canaria. In F. Morales Padrón (Ed.), *Canarias: Crónicas de su conquista. Transcripción, estudio y notas,* (2nd ed., pp. 383–468). Las Palmas de Gran Canaria (Spain): Ediciones del Cabildo Insular de Gran Canaria. Las Palmas de Gran Canaria.

González Antón, R., & Arco Aguilar, M. C. (2007). *Los enamorados de la osa menor. Navegación y pesca en la protohistoria de Canarias. Colección Canarias Arqueológica* (Vol. 1). Santa Cruz de Tenerife (Spain): Cabildo de Tenerife.

Ireland, T. (2010). Excavating Globalization from the Ruins of Colonialism: Archaeological Heritage Management Responses to Cultural Change. ICOMOS Scientific Symposium Changing World, Changing Views of Heritage: The Impact of Global Change on Cultural Heritage. http://www.international.icomos.org/adcom/dublin2010/Paper_2.pdf. Accessed 15 Jan 2013.

Kratochwil, G. (1999). Some observations on the First Amazigh World Congress (27–30 August, Tafira, Canary Islands). *Die Welt Des Islams, 39*(2), 149–158.

Lydon, J., & Rizvi, U. (Eds.). (2010). *Handbook of postcolonial archaeology.* Walnut Creek, California: Left Coast Press.

Maddy-Weitzman, B. (2006). Ethno-politics and globalisation in North Africa: The berber culture movement. *The Journal of North African Studies, 11,* 71–83.

Maddy-Weitzman, B. (2012). *The berber identity movement and the challenge to North African states.* Austin: University of Texas Press.

Mauss, M. (1989 [1947]). *Manual de etnografía (Manuel d'ethnographie)* (3rd ed.). Mexico: Fondo de Cultura Económica.

Mederos Martín, A., & Escribano Cobo, G. (2002). *Los aborígenes y la prehistoria de Canarias.* Santa Cruz de Tenerife (Spain): Centro de la Cultura Popular Canaria.

Pérez Guartambel, C. (2006). *Justicia indígena. Facultad de Jurisprudencia de la Universidad de Cuenca*. Ecuador: Colegio de Abogados del Azuay.

Ramos Martín, J. (2012). La construcción del bereber: historiografía y colonialismo en el siglo XIX. In R. González Zalacaín (Ed.), Actas de las III Jornadas "Prebendado Pacheco" de investigación histórica (pp. 93–118). Santa Cruz de Tenerife (Spain): Ilustre Ayuntamiento de la Villa de Tegueste

Sabir, A. (2008). *Las Canarias prehispánicas y el Norte de África. El ejemplo de Marruecos. Paralelismos lingüísticos y culturales*. Rabat: Institut Royal de la Culture Amazighe

Said, E. W. (1997). *Orientalismo (Orientalism)*. Barcelona: Editorial De Bolsillo

Stevens Arroyo, A. M. (1997). Canary Islands and the Antillian. In A. Tejera Gaspar (Ed.), *La sorpresa de Europa. (El encuentro de culturas). Documentos congresuales* (pp. 83–107). La Laguna (Spain): Servicio de Publicaciones de la Universidad de La Laguna

Tejera Gaspar, A. (2001). *Las religiones preeuropeas de las Islas Canarias*. Madrid: Ediciones del Orto.

Tejera Gaspar, A., & González Antón, R. (1987). *Las Culturas aborígenes canarias*. Santa Cruz de Tenerife: Interinsular Canaria

Tilmatine, M. (2008). *Los estudios amaziges. Bibliografía temática*. Barcelona: Ediciones Bellaterra. UNED-Melilla

Trigger, B. (2006). *A history of archaeological thought* (2nd ed.). Cambridge: Cambridge University Press.

Veracini, L. (2006). A prehistory of Australia's history wars: The evolution of aboriginal history during the 1970s and 1980s. *Australian Journal of Politics and History, 52*(Issue 3), 439–468.

Willems, J. H. W. (2012). World heritage and global heritage: The tip of the Iceberg. In A. Castillo (Ed.), *Actas del Primer Congreso Internacional de Buenas Prácticas en Patrimonio Mundial: Arqueología*. Menorca, 9–13 de abril de 2012, (pp. 36–50). Madrid: Editora Complutense. https://portal.ucm.es/web/publicaciones/congresos. Accessed 29 Jan 2013.

Chapter 2
The Invention of Canarian Prehistory and Early Archaeological Heritage Management in the Nineteenth Century (1868–1936)

At the end of the seventeenth century, following the gradual disappearance of the indigenous Canarians and their culture, their legacy began to be viewed from an archaeological rather than an ethnographic perspective, as previously noted. European authors between the fourteenth century and most of the seventeenth century were not interested in archaeological information regarding the indigenous Canarian world, inasmuch as the information they possessed referred to surviving native populations who were therefore ethnographic subjects rather than fossils. This explains why no studies were conducted in the Canary Islands similar to those produced by antiquarians in Europe (Trigger 2006, p. 22), in which research into (archaeological) material evidence supplemented studies based on written documents. Therefore, archaeological interest in the indigenous past began in the Canary Islands only in the second half of the eighteenth century and was based on searching for and collecting Guanche remains. It was common practice among the wealthy, who could afford the luxury of purchasing objects belonging to the indigenous culture, to possess a mummy, skeleton, or skull of an indigenous Canarian which they kept in their study to display to friends (Diego 1953, p. 136). These ítems were sold by looters to the Canarian and even foreign collectors, destroying the potential for future archaeological research.

2.1 The First Archaeological Collections

During this period there was no need for archaeological excavations in the Canary Islands, because Guanche funerals usually took place in natural caves where the corpse and provisions were deposited, whether mummified or not, without being buried.[1]

The interest in Canarian antiquities did not become widespread until the early nineteenth century. The first collections were assembled in the first half of the century, namely the Juan de Megliorini y Spínola and Gabinete o Museo Casilda de Tacoronte collections, both in Tenerife, the Instituto de Canarias de La Laguna collection, also

---

[1] On the variety and types of indigenous Canarian burials, see the work of Arco (1977 and 1992–1993).

A. J. Farrujia de la Rosa, *An archaeology of the margins,*
SpringerBriefs in Archaeology, DOI 10.1007/978-1-4614-9396-9_2,
© The Author(s) 2014

in Tenerife, which had a Natural History Museum with a large number of indigenous skulls and bone remains, several ceramic vessels, a millstone, and a mummy, and the Conde de la Vega Grande collection in Gran Canaria. Some years later, in 1874, the Tenerife scholar Anselmo J. Benítez founded the Villa Benítez Museum in Santa Cruz de Tenerife (Farrujia 2010, Chap. 3).

In their time, these archaeological collections were considered museums, given that they were designed to be visited. However, although they contained some interesting items and archaeological remains from indigenous Canarian settlements, they should not be considered actual museums but simply collections of antiquities and curios assembled by their owners, who usually had no academic training, as Ramírez (1997, p. 312) and Mederos (2003, p. 196) have noted. The creation of these collections explicitly reveals an archaeological interest in the material culture of the indigenous Canarians and, above all, in anthropological remains, whether mummified or not. They were not, therefore, balanced collections, inasmuch as they were created randomly, according to circumstances and the criteria set by their owners. Moreover, they were created essentially by the aristocracy and the middle class, unlike the situation in mainland Spain where the Catholic Church also played an important role in the study of antiquities.

In the Iberian peninsula, many convents and monasteries treasured archaeological items for centuries, and many important personalities of the Catholic Church, such as Fidel Fita and Colomé (1835–1918), among others, played a crucial role in the study of antiquities, studying the history of the Iberian peninsula in antiquity, and especially everything related to the indigenous population (Maier 2003; Ayarzagüena 2004). But in the Canary Islands, the role of the Catholic Church in archeology was marginal, practically nonexistent. The Canarian indigenous cultures were classified as Neolithic and studied mainly from the naturalistic paradigm. Consequently, the research in prehistoric archeology, whose central axis was the antiquity of man, was developed by members of the liberal bourgeoisie, who belonged to liberal institutions, such as El Museo Canario. The active participation of the Catholic Church was basically limited to the dialectical opposition to Darwin's evolutionism, in the second half of the nineteenth century, a panorama that is clearly in contrast with the active role played by the religious in the Canaries in previous centuries. The Dominican Fray Alonso de Espinosa (1594) and the Franciscan Fray José de Sosa (1678) paid attention in their respective books to the study and description of the Canarian indigenous societies (Farrujia 2010).

As previously noted, the development of archaeological collections centered mainly on Tenerife and Gran Canaria or, in other words, the "central" islands in the archipelago, where cultural, economic, and social development was more extensive. In the case of Lanzarote and Fuerteventura, for example, centuries of isolation and a poor, arid, and sparsely populated environment had contributed towards a lack of appreciation of cultural assets (Cabrera 1996, p. 15). In the case of islands such as La Gomera there is no information on these initial stages of Canarian archaeology. In El Hierro archaeology became more important after the rediscovery of the El Júlan rock engravings in 1873. In the case of La Palma the first archaeological news is also related to rock art, namely the Cueva de Belmaco engravings, discovered at the end of the eighteenth century (Farrujia 2009 and 2010, Chap. 8).

This fragmented and uneven scenario shows that, in terms of culture, the Canary Islands have had to confront an unusual geographical situation, namely their remoteness from the major centers of communication, particularly in the case of the more peripheral islands such as Lanzarote, Fuerteventura, and El Hierro. The culture that developed on the islands has, in historical terms, had to deal with the discontinuity of an (island) territory that has, until recently, suffered from poor communications. In other words, the intellectual and creative Canarian culture had to confront both an "interior" and an "exterior" context that had conflicting meanings.

2.2 The Beginning of Prehistoric Archaeology in the Canary Islands

In the Canary Islands it was not until the second half of the nineteenth century that archaeology, as the "science of objects" and fieldwork, began to develop. This was due to the development of prehistoric studies in western Europe and, in part, the relationship that had been established between the Cro-Magnon race and the indigenous Canarians (Farrujia 2004, p. 251). In these initial stages of Canarian archaeology, French influence is clear, both in the direct involvement of French authors in the islands and in the influence that many of them had on Canarian intellectuals, as well as the fact that some of the latter had trained in France.

Moreover, the archaeological studies developed at the time in France, Germany, or England cannot be understood without taking into account the economic, political, and social changes that emerged in Europe as a result of the Industrial Revolution and which affected its genesis and the development of the emerging disciplines of archaeology and anthropology, both closely linked to the bourgeois sectors of society. In the case of the Canary Islands, the impact of economic factors (a crisis or boom in particular crops, the establishment of free ports in 1852,[2] the trade revival, etc.) led to the configuration and consolidation of a capitalist economy, turning the (landowning and merchant) bourgeoisie into the ruling social class and, as in the rest of Europe, the sector of society most interested in archaeological and anthropological studies.

The leading geostrategic role played by the archipelago itself in the colonial division of Africa by the European powers is also a factor that should be taken into consideration in analyzing Canarian archaeological studies, because the complex web of annexionist and colonial interests ultimately made the islands an enclave coveted by the European powers. This would, in fact, lead to the development of a colonialist archaeology with racist undertones in the Canary Islands, in which certain foreign authors associated with Canarian studies collaborated (Farrujia 2005).

---

[2] The establishment of free ports allowed the Canary Islands a significant level of openness to the outside world and broad scope to adapt to international economic change. This measure involved the liberalization of the entry and exit of goods in the archipelago, stimulating the island economy and creating an important fiscal incentive for trade with, and by, the islands. Free ports favored banana and tomato exports to Europe from the end of the nineteenth century. In terms of archaeological studies, it fostered links between the Canary Islands and Europe and the subsequent arrival of scientific publications, mainly from France and England. Canarian intellectuals could therefore have access to the leading archaeological literature of the time.

2.3   The Cro-Magnon Race and the System of the Four Ages

In 1837 the stratigraphic excavation of the Abbeville archaeological site, led by the pioneer of French prehistory Boucher Crèvecoeur de Perthes, and the subsequent publication of the findings in 1860, inaugurated a phase in prehistoric science that was characterized by the discovery of "antediluvian man." However, the main advances in Palaeolithic archaeology took place after 1860, when the number of prehistoric excavations increased and the findings were published in the *Revue archéologique* and in *Matériaux*, placing particular importance on the discoveries made in river terraces in the north of the country. The most relevant of these—particularly because of its repercussions for the Canary Islands—occurred in 1868, when Louis Lartet (1840–1899) discovered at the Cro-Magnon site (Les Eyzies, Dordogne) the remains of five members of this race. Armed with this material evidence, the studies then aimed to determine how long these humans had lived in the area and whether evolutionist traits could be detected as early as the Paleolithic period (Gran-Aymerich 2001, p. 196). However, it was not until 1867 that the engineer Gabriel de Mortillet developed a system similar to that of John Lubbock to define four ages: the Flaked Stone Age, the Polished Stone Age, the Bronze Age, and the Iron Age. As already argued, Mortillet's classification was based on a typology for tools and artifacts, which were organized into periods.[3] Thus Mortillet defined a program of study based on a notion of the global, linear, and universal progress of the human species, in which biological and cultural evolution were parallel (Coye 2004, p. 5). The system of the four ages was therefore defined by a system of organization based on artifacts and the ability to construct relative chronologies from archaeological data using seriation and stratigraphy.

2.3.1   1868: The Cro-Magnon Race and Prehistoric Archaeology in the Canary Islands

As previously noted, in 1868 Luis Lartet discovered fossilized Cro-Magnon remains. A few years later in 1871, Paul Broca advised that there were morphological similarities between some of the Canarian skulls in the Bouglinval collection in the École des Hautes Études, which had come from the Barranco Hondo site (Tenerife), and those of Cro-Magnon man. Another French anthropologist, Théodore Hamy (1842–1908), agreed with Broca, which led Quatrefages to write to Sabin Berthelot (1794–1880), the French consul in the Canary Islands at the time, asking for more material to be sent for him to study with the aim of confirming this possible link (Farrujia 2010, Chap. 3). However, in 1874, without having received the material they had requested, the French authors, Quatrefages and Hamy published a summary of their work *Crania ethnica, les crânes des races humaines* in the *Bulletin of the Anthropological Society of Paris*, based on a study of the distribution of the Cro-Magnon fossil remains identified thus far. The authors pointed out the differences that existed between the Neanderthals and the Cro-Magnon race and confirmed the

---

[3] The notion of "period" is directly related to "industry," prefiguring the concept of culture.

presence of the Cro-Magnon type—whose main settlement had been established in the Vézère region—in France, Holland, Italy, and Tenerife (Quatrefages and Hamy 1874).[4] Despite having identified the presence of this Quaternary race in the Canary Islands, it was not until 1877 that Berthelot sent 10 skulls that had come from El Hierro and Gran Canaria to Paris, which explains why the expected characteristics of the Cro-Magnon race could not be clearly defined until then. This led to Quatrefages, on March 22nd, 1876, commissioning René Verneau (1852–1938) to undertake an exhaustive investigation, resulting in his scientific mission to the Canary Islands. René Pierre Verneau was a professor at the National Museum of Natural History and the Institute of Human Paleontology, curator of the Museum of Ethnography, president of the French Institute of Archaeology and editor-in-chief of the journal *Anthropologie*.

Verneau's contribution was to systematize all the anthropological data, using recently discovered methods and working from a broad archaeological–ethnological base. This enabled him to discover an important part of what later researchers would echo: large numbers of Cro-Magnon individuals, especially in La Gomera and Tenerife and striking differences in the Gran Canaria population. However, he had little material, in particular skulls, to work with and his publications were based on only a part of the material he collected. Moreover, he never fully revised the El Museo Canario collection in Las Palmas (discussed later) a collection that Verneau himself had assembled and organized.

Verneau also defined the indigenous culture in terms of mega-elements (dolmens or sepulchers in caves), which contributed towards creating an excessively simplistic vision of the cultures being studied. In addition, the influence of anthropological arguments on his work overshadowed the role that sociocultural factors may have played as defining elements in the societies being studied. The excavations he personally undertook, which essentially focused on recovering bone remains, usually skulls, also contributed towards undervaluing evidence based on artifacts as well as the archaeological context itself, thus diminishing a good deal of the archaeological potential of the Canary Islands (Farrujia 2004). It is also important to note that a wealth of archaeological and anthropological material (essentially bone remains, the remains of mummies, ceramics, lithic tools, and paintings), was sent by Verneau to the Musée de l'Homme in Paris (Farrujia 2005). The looting of the Canarian archaeological heritage since the end of the seventeenth century is also reflected in travel literature. The most coveted items were mummies (Farrujia 2004, Chap. 11).

Verneau's view of the dispersal of the Cro-Magnon race contributed towards defending French imperialist interests in Africa and the Canary Islands, proceeding in the same way as his compatriots Faidherbe, Tissot, and Broca, among others. Reflecting the ethnocentric world view of the time, the expansion of the Cro-Magnon race beyond French territory implied that all the areas occupied by the said Quaternary race would have been populated in ancient times by the ancestors of the Gallic nation (Farrujia 2005). It should be noted that, according the observations of Quatrefages himself in an 1873 article entitled "*La Science et la Patrie*" (published in the

---

[4] Within a few years the work of Quatrefages and Hamy had established Cro-Magnon man as the archetypal representative of the human race in the age of the reindeer (Upper Paleolithic era).

Bulletin of the *Association française pour l'avancement des sciences*), the scientist is a soldier, a well-educated population is a well-armed population, and scientific work should bring the joys of patriotism to a country. It was this patriotism, in fact, that would lead to the recognition, in 1889 of the Paris School of Anthropology as a public institution and to Gabriel de Mortillet writing the *Formation de la nation française* (1897; Blanckaert 2001, p. 19).

French scientific intervention in the Canary Islands (led by authors such as Sabin Berthelot and René Verneau) and the actual scientific contacts established between Canarian and French authors meant that Gallic archaeology became the model that was followed in the islands, both from a theoretical and a methodological point of view. It should be remembered that Sabin Berthelot lived in Tenerife for over 25 years and published some of his articles in local journals such as the *Revista de Canarias*, while also keeping in written contact with the Canarian intellectuals of the time. At the same time, René Verneau spent several periods in the El Museo Canario in Las Palmas de Gran Canaria, where he studied its collection of anthropological and archaeological material and published the results of some of his work in the *Revista El Museo Canario*. In addition, French scientific publications (both archaeological and anthropological) circulated widely throughout the islands, as can be seen from the bibliographies used by Canarian authors (Farrujia 2010, Chap. 3).

With regard to these scientific contacts, it should also be remembered that Canarian authors such as Juan Bethencourt Alfonso (1847–1913) and Rosendo García Ramos y Bretillard (1834–1913), had been to Paris, where they had visited academies and offices and established contacts, which were continued in the form of letters when they returned to the islands, with leading scientists of the time, such as Armand de Quatrefages, Teodore Hamy, and Paul Broca (Farrujia 2004). The Canarian author Dr. Gregorio Chil y Naranjo (1831–1901) first became associated with French academic circles when he studied medicine at the Sorbonne University (Paris) from 1849 to 1859. Subsequently, he met Broca, Quatrefages, Hamy, Topinard, Verneau, and a couple of years later Gabriel de Mortillet, which helped to keep him up to date with the latest scientific developments. Chil was also familiar with the work of biologists such as Darwin (1859), physical anthropologists such as Broca, and prehistorians such as Boucher de Perthes (1847–1857), Mortillet (1872, 1882), and Lubbock (1865); in other words, he had read all the French and English authors who had helped disseminate evolutionist arguments throughout Europe. Through these friendships he was also able to attend various congresses and scientific exhibitions held in France, such as the conferences organized in Lille (1874) and Nantes (1875) by the *Association française pour l'Avancement des Sciences*.

2.3.2   The Influence of the French Model in the Canary Islands

This background meant that from a very early stage the principles of French prehistoric archaeology were assimilated in the Canary Islands, and that artifacts became the key to explaining the cultural evolution of the islands, on the basis of a combination of evolutionary and diffusionist theories. This explains why the Canarian authors

Fig. 2.1 Ceramic idols on display in El Museo Canario at the end of the nineteenth century, associated with the "prehistoric" phase. Photograph: Institute de Paléontologie Humaine (Paris)

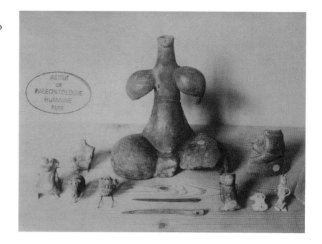

would argue, on the basis of evolutionism and diffusionism, for the existence of the Stone Age in the Canary Islands. The physical location of the Canary Islands (as an archipelago in the Atlantic) meant that the first settlers would have arrived there by sea from a foreign base or center of diffusion, hence the coexistence of evolutionist and diffusionist theories in the Canarian archipelago in the nineteenth century.

Chil y Naranjo and Agustín Millares Torres (1826–1896), for example, claimed that there had been a crudely carved flint age in the Canary Islands (Chil y Naranjo 1876, p. 5; Millares 1893, p. 185), thus equating one of the prehistoric periods of the islands with one of the stages in French prehistory defined by Mortillet (the Flaked Stone Age). In addition, Chil y Naranjo (1876), Millares Torres (1893), and Bethencourt Alfonso (1912) argued for the existence of a Neolithic period in the Canary Islands on the basis of the existence of polished tools (associated with the Neolithic) and rough pottery in the archaeological records for the islands and the fact that the indigenous Canarians were cave dwellers. The presence of bone tools in Canarian sites also led Carlos Pizarroso y Belmonte (1841–1916) to associate the Guanches of Tenerife with the third Stone Age, known as the *Aurignac* by Mortillet and defined by a substantial increase in objects manufactured from bone (Pizarroso 1880, p. 68; Fig. 2.1).

The definition of the different ages in French prehistory was based on stratigraphy and seriation, but the situation was very different in the Canary Islands, where only artifacts were used. The lack of stratigraphic evidence from Canarian sites in comparison to French sites and, above all, the actual inability of Canarian intellectuals to recognize the existence of archaeological stratigraphy in situ, are the main factors that explain the pre-eminence of material evidence and the total absence of references to the existence of archaeological stratigraphy. Consequently, nineteenth-century Canarian archaeology contained an important internal contradiction: although they had no relative chronology based on stratigraphy, artifacts were used to define the cultural sequence for Canarian prehistory. Typology was therefore the methodological tool used to establish diachrony in Canarian prehistory, inasmuch as it was the differences observed in the form and technology of the artifacts that enabled them to be classified in sequential order, before or after each other.

Fig. 2.2 Indigenous and
historic (ethnographic)
ceramics from Gran Canaria
on display in El Museo
Canario at the end of the
nineteenth century. The
indigenous ceramics, made
by hand without the use of a
wheel, were considered
"prehistoric" by
nineteenth-century
researchers. Photograph:
Teodoro Maisch

In excavating archaeological sites, the different Canarian authors proceeded more in the manner of antiquarians than archaeologists, because they focused only on recovering material evidence, therefore marginalizing or undervaluing any information that could be obtained from the archaeological context itself. This interest in archaeological objects purely for their aesthetic qualities did not require any rigorous methodology for documenting the concrete circumstances of the find. In those days sites were literally "emptied" in the search for objects, many of which were ignored, together with the related sedimentological and structural details (stratigraphy). This was also common practice among Spanish mainland archaeologists (Lull and Micó 1997, p. 114) and other contemporary European archaeologists (Schnapp 2002, p. 135; Fig. 2.2).

At the same time, the firm belief in unilinear evolutionism (combined, in the case of the Canary Islands, with diffusionism) led the same Canarian authors to refer to the existence of megaliths (dolmens) in the Canary Islands that were related to those in France (such as the l'Ardeche dolmen). From this, it was concluded that the indigenous Canarians had existed since the Quaternary period and therefore since the paleontological era of the great mammals.

However, contrary to the opinions of Chil, Pizarroso, and Bethencourt, there are no archaeological records of any dolmens in the Canary Islands. With regard to this fact, it should be borne in mind that megalithic monuments (dolmens and tombs)—one of the first prehistoric phenomena to attract the attention of enthusiasts—were frequently confused in the nineteenth century with merely unstable stones and natural cavities, while at the same time the wildest theories emerged to explain their existence. From this it may be deduced that in the era in which Chil and Bethencourt were writing there was no empirical capacity to distinguish between anthropic megalithic structures and simple nonanthropic geological formations (Farrujia 2002, p. 43), which may account for the erroneous assessments made by both authors. The influence of unilinear evolutionism on these scholars should also be noted, leading them to establish forced archaeological comparisons between the Canarian and French contexts (Fig. 2.3).

Fig. 2.3 Indigenous
Cro-Magnon skulls on display
in El Museo Canario at the
end of the nineteenth century.
Photograph: Teodoro Maisch

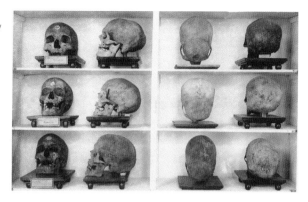

Together with evidence based on artifacts and megaliths, the presence of the Cro-Magnon race in the archipelago was another of the arguments employed by the Canarian authors of the time to attribute a Neolithic culture to the indigenous people or Guanches. It should also be borne in mind that during the nineteenth century scientific contacts with France meant that Canarian anthropology, following the methodology and theoretical principles of French physical anthropology, adopted raciology wholesale as the main approach to studying the indigenous population. Yet, whereas in France the scarcity of archaeological data meant that archaeologists resorted to the conclusions drawn by physical anthropologists, linguists, and ethnologists on the assumption that ethnology revealed almost everything they wanted to know about prehistoric times, in the Canary Islands the situation was very different, because physical anthropology and the actual ethnohistorical sources were used to supplement archaeological information.

The lack of bronze and iron tools in the archaeological records perused by the nineteenth-century Canarian authors led them to reject the idea of a Bronze Age and an Iron Age in the Canary Islands. The fact that the indigenous Canarians were defined as a "rudimentary civilization" is symptomatic of this approach (Chil y Naranjo 1876, p. 10).

In short, the contacts between French and Canarian intellectuals and the relationship established early on between the indigenous Canarians and the Cro-Magnon race and consequently between the Canary Islands and French prehistory, were factors that ensured the success of the French frame of reference. Nor should it be forgotten that the archaeology and anthropology of the time were respected because they had been developed in France (and also in England), the international center of political, economic, and cultural development at the time (Trigger 2006, p. 107). Due to its prestige, the archaeology of the Paleolithic period provided a model for the study of prehistory in Western Europe and therefore in the Canary Islands (Fig. 2.4).

In applying external criteria to the Canary Islands, indigenous Canarian cultures were treated as if they shared the same evolutionary development as other parts of Africa or Europe. In this sense, the cultural evolutionist models simplified the indigenous Canarian societies, as they did other past societies (Johnson 2000, p. 178). Thus the particularities or specific features of individual cultures were not considered important. Moreover, the evolutionist cultural models took neither contingency nor

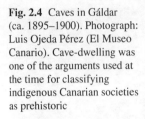

Fig. 2.4 Caves in Gáldar (ca. 1895–1900). Photograph: Luis Ojeda Pérez (El Museo Canario). Cave-dwelling was one of the arguments used at the time for classifying indigenous Canarian societies as prehistoric

historical accident into account, giving the impression that all societies evolved inexorably into states. Finally, it should be remembered that the European evolutionist archaeology and anthropology developed in Africa after colonial partitioning or, in other words, after the Berlin Conference of 1884–1885, was a clear example of European imperialistic interventionism. In this sense, the French archaeology developed in the Canary Islands at the end of the nineteenth century was clearly influenced by colonial interests and motivations, because evolutionist theories provided, among other things, a justification for European superiority and its consequent colonial domination of Africa and the Canary Islands (Farrujia 2005).

The main consequence of this was the inevitable adoption of French scientific premises by Canarian authors and thus the development of an ethnocentric view of the indigenous Canarians.

It is striking that the prehistoric archaeology developed in mainland Spain had no impact on the Canary Islands. This may be explained by the fact that prehistoric archaeology had started some years earlier in the Iberian peninsula at the beginning of the 1860s, the lack of any significant contact between academic circles on the mainland and in the Canary Islands in terms of the emergence of prehistoric studies in the islands, the lack of interest in Canarian issues on the part of mainland authors, and the actual synchrony in the development of prehistoric archaeology in the Iberian peninsula and in the Canary Islands, because in both cases the first publications were inspired by the French model, which quickly became the frame of reference.

2.4 Archaeological Heritage Management in the Nineteenth Century

As previously noted, it was the bourgeois intellectuals on the islands who adopted the main theoretical principles that lay behind the scientific advances of the time and were considered necessary, not only in order to understand society but, more important, to create new policies to improve social development. Regenerationism, positivism, and evolutionism were the focal points of reflection and gave rise to bitter controversy, which was at times more political than scientific.

It was from this environment that the institutions dedicated to the preservation of the cultural and biological heritage of the indigenous Canarians first emerged: El Gabinete Científico, El Museo Canario, and the Sociedad La Cosmológica. They all drew on anthropological and archaeological research on the Guanches, in the form of a certain amount of fieldwork on the various islands, as previously discussed. One fundamental characteristic of these institutions was that, although their objectives included an essentially heritage conservation concept in terms of the Guanche archaeological and ethnographic collections, they were all designed to serve more as research centers, in particular El Museo Canario. This required archives and libraries and the opportunity to carry out individual research, as reflected in the expeditions and excavations undertaken by their members.

2.4.1 El Gabinete Científico (Santa Cruz de Tenerife)

In September 1877, the *Gabinete Científico* was founded in Santa Cruz de Tenerife, an institution that was to play a leading role in the development of anthropology and archaeology in the western Canary Islands (Tenerife, La Palma, La Gomera, and El Hierro) under the leadership of Juan Bethencourt Alfonso. The institution was established as an annex to the *Establecimiento de Segunda Enseñanza* due to the need for a museum that would provide practical training for students at the Institute. From the outset it was involved in developing a series of archaeological and anthropological activities organized by Bethencourt himself. He supervised the work of a wide range of collaborators who, acting almost as partners, provided the institution with the archaeological materials it needed. There is evidence of the contribution made by Ramón Gómez, for example, a collaborator in Puerto de La Cruz, who sent 120 Guanche skulls to the *Gabinete. El Gabinete* was also supported by collaborators in La Gomera and Fuerteventura and when materials had to be collected from islands where there was no staff, Bethencourt Alfonso himself went there. There are records of his field trips to La Palma and El Hierro, as well as Gran Canaria and Lanzarote (Diego 1982, p. 9; Ramírez 1997, p. 314).

As stipulated in its 1878 Regulations, the *Gabinete* objectives included "the study of natural science and, in particular, natural science in the Canarian Archipelago" (p. 2) and therefore the study of the prehistoric anthropology and archaeology of the Canary Islands. As a result of its work under the leadership of Bethencourt Alfonso, over 500 skulls, several mummies, and specific items associated with the indigenous material culture (44 millstones, vessels, fish hooks, and 18 spears and shepherd's crooks) were collected in Tenerife. The *Gabinete* also housed collections donated by, among others, Sr. Lebrun and Juan de la Puerta Canseco.

Among members of the *Gabinete*, special mention should be made of Juan Bethencourt Alfonso, Rosendo García Ramos, and Carlos Pizarroso y Belmonte, due to the

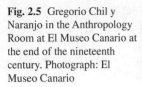

Fig. 2.5 Gregorio Chil y Naranjo in the Anthropology Room at El Museo Canario at the end of the nineteenth century. Photograph: El Museo Canario

contributions they made to the study of the indigenous Canarian world. They all published in the *Revista de Canarias* and other periodicals and formed the so-called "Scientific Generation of 1880."

After the death of Bethencourt Alfonso, followed by Rosendo García Ramos, the apathy and lack of skills of the other members and staff led to the decline of the *Gabinete*, whose collections were subsequently added to the Bernabé Rodríguez collection and the Anthropology and Natural History Museum in Santa Cruz de Tenerife, which was founded on December 31st, 1902.

2.4.2   *El Museo Canario (Las Palmas de Gran Canaria)*

In Gran Canaria there was a similar development, in terms of museology, although given the limited future prospects for Tenerife organizations, the outlook was more promising. In September 1879 a group of intellectuals headed by Dr. Gregorio Chil y Naranjo met with the aim of founding a scientific society that was later christened *El Museo Canario.* It was inaugurated in 1880 and had its headquarters on the second floor of the Las Palmas de Gran Canaria City Hall. The work of the institution has continued, despite some setbacks, up to the present day (Fig. 2.5).

The main aim of the society was to create a museum and library that would serve to develop and advance popular instruction, as well as the special study of subjects related to the Canary Islands and its products. It consisted of a museum, a study, a library, archives, and a regular periodical, the *El Museo Canario* scientific journal. It also organized cultural evenings and scientific–literary meetings involving speeches, discussions, and lectures and public conferences. As such, *El Museo Canario*, founded in a city that had no secondary education facilities or university, became the driving force behind higher education and scientific advancement in its particular field.

The first materials were gathered by Chil himself and by Victor Grau-Bassas (1847–1918), who organized trips to the interior and southern areas of the island to recover mummies, fabrics, and indigenous ceramics, although without following any scientific method. Together with the work developed by Bethencourt Alfonso, essentially in Tenerife, this marked the beginnings of the first fieldwork in the Canary Islands that was in any sense systematic, from the 1870s onwards. The bulk of the El Museo Canario collection consisted of items discovered on field expeditions carried out by its members. However, there were also some important donations, such as the collection belonging to Don Fernando del Castillo Westerling, the Count of Vega Grande who, before he died, commissioned his children to entrust to the museum certain objects he had collected, mainly in the Arguineguin, Mogán, and Guayadeque areas, which were associated with the early inhabitants of Gran Canaria. In 1901 the Museum received a complete mummy, painted ceramic vessels, rush fabrics, and several idols (Millares 1901).

In *El Museo Canario* it was Gregorio Chil y Naranjo and, to a lesser extent, Agustín Millares Torres, who played a significant role in the study of the indigenous Canarians. From the point of view of schools of thought, evolutionism clearly predominated in the ideas of these two authors and within the institution founded by Chil. Their uncompromising defense of unilinear evolutionism would lead both to argue for the existence of the Paleolithic and Neolithic ages in the Canary Islands, as previously discussed. The importance of Chil y Naranjo, however, did not only lie in his individual work but also in his efforts to mobilize local intellectuals and scientists and in his contacts with European circles. In this sense, his most important project was the founding of *El Museo Canario*. Chil's objective was to introduce a solid line of research and suitable resources for the preservation of the historical–archaeological–ethnographic heritage that would enable El Museo Canario to become the main cultural center on the islands (Reglamento 1879; Farrujia 2005; Ortiz 2005, p. 214; Fig. 2.6).

2.4.3 Sociedad La Cosmológica (Santa Cruz de La Palma)

The island of La Palma also had its own scientific institution, the *Sociedad La Cosmológica*, founded in 1881. As can be seen from the first volume of its statutes, it was clearly influenced by the El Museo Canario model,

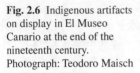

Fig. 2.6 Indigenous artifacts on display in El Museo Canario at the end of the nineteenth century. Photograph: Teodoro Maisch

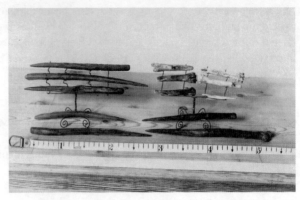

> The main objective of this association is to found a Museum of Natural History and Ethnography for the study of these subjects in general and the geological, faunal and floral products associated with the Guanches in particular. (Reglamento..., 1881)

Article 2 added that "no discussion of political or religious matters is permitted, unless in a purely speculative sense." This clearly indicates that the leading intellectuals in the society were far more conservative in political and religious terms, inasmuch as many other contemporary island and mainland centers dedicated to scientific debate affirmed their inalienable right to freedom of thought in understanding natural phenomena.

The Regulations also established that the society should be "founded on the basis of items donated to the Museum by members or individuals and those which may be purchased with funds from the Society." The archaeology section dedicated to the Guanches was in fact stocked with donations from private individuals and museums, in addition to items discovered during fieldwork carried out by the members. It consisted of ceramics, lithic tools, skulls, and other bones and was regularly supplemented by the results of the members' research work in archaeological sites on the island.[5]

The *Cosmológica* Regulations bear the signature of its first president, Abelardo González Martínez, and its first headquarters were provided by the *Sociedad Económica de Amigos del País*, although they were not suitable for the work of the society. It subsequently moved to a house in Calle Cuna where the museum was opened to the public on January 23rd, 1887. In 1889 the Society moved again to the premises where it has remained to the present day, in the *Pósito Municipal* or *Casa Panera* building (Ortiz 2005, p. 221).

The contribution made by La *Cosmológica* to the study of the indigenous culture was modest, amounting to no more than the simple acquisition of archaeological

---

[5] In 1983, 100 years after it was founded, La Cosmológica, which remained a private society, donated its museum to the Island Council and its collections form the basis of the Archaeology and Natural History section of the *Museo Insular del Cabildo de La Palma*.

Fig. 2.7 Antiquities Room at the Sociedad La Cosmológica at the end of the nineteenth century. Photograph: Sociedad La Cosmológica archives

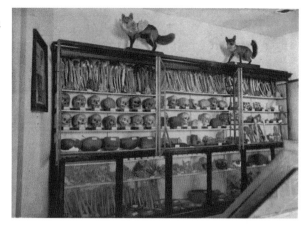

and anthropological items and involving no underlying methodology other than opportunity. Moreover, it was more provincial in scope than El Museo Canario or the Gabinete Científico. Its members had less understanding of ideas and less distinguished scientific and academic backgrounds, and served more as promoters and disseminators of local culture than authentic creators of ideas and specific discourses on the cultural and human history of the archipelago and their own island. One leading figure within the institution, due to his work and legacy, was Antonio Rodríguez López (1836–1901), the author of works such as *Consideraciones sobre el Darwinismo* (1881) and *Los Bereberes del Riff* (1881), which reveal his creationist position and rejection of Darwinism, condemning its "atheist materialism" and arguing that religion was the basis of all institutions (Farrujia 2010, Chap. 3; Fig. 2.7).

2.5 Protection of the Archaeological Patrimony in the Legal Vacuum of the Nineteenth Century

The archaeological situation in the Canary Islands in the nineteenth century, in common with the situation on the Spanish mainland, suffered from a lack of legislation to cover excavation and antiquities. However, efforts were made to improve the archaeological methodology for fieldwork and conservation of the archaeological patrimony. The 1878 Regulations of *El Gabinete Científico* in Santa Cruz de Tenerife placed particular emphasis on the correct documentation of archaeological assets, stating that it was necessary to provide a detailed report of finds and "include references for mummies, skeletons, skulls, bones etc. belonging to the ancient races of these islands, describing, if possible and in as much detail as possible, the location and condition in which they were found" (Reglamento. . . , 1878, p. 6). The Regulations did not cover any matters relating to the handling and preservation of items, as was also the case in other European museums (Schnapp 2002).

The *El Museo Canario* Regulations, approved on March 26th, 1886, expressed a greater concern for the preservation of archaeological assets, referring specifically to the role of the curator, a position held in the early years by Víctor Grau Bassas, an excellent anatomist who, together with Diego Ripoche, was responsible for organizing the exhibits in the museum rooms. Article Six of the Statutes stipulates that it was necessary to keep a book of records containing detailed descriptions of the finds so that each item that arrived at the museum would be fully documented with descriptions, sketches, and drawings and the scientific value of the items would be enhanced. In addition it emphasized that there should be "the most accurate description of the objects found, the place where they were found and their origins, with orographic and physical data if necessary." Articles Seven and Eight covered the work of the museum curator, stating that he should strive to take good care of the items and provide information "on their merits and importance" (Chil y Naranjo 1886).

These measures made it possible gradually to build up archaeological knowledge of the Canary Islands by documenting new and previously unknown finds and acquiring archaeological items that were housed and preserved in the *El Gabinete Científico* and *El Museo Canario* collections. However, given the lack of any adequate methodology and the attitude of the antiquarians involved in the work, the archaeological context of the items that were acquired was marginalized. In addition, both sets of regulations had little practical application and did not extend beyond the circle of scholars and intellectuals connected with the institutions.

2.6 The 1911 Law on Excavations and Antiquities

The aforementioned legal vacuum in the nineteenth-century would not be remedied until 1911 with the *Law of 7th June on Excavations and Antiquities* and the regulations for its application, which were approved on March 1st, 1912. This law prescribed regulations for artistic and scientific excavations and for the conservation of ruins and antiquities and may be seen as the first major Spanish law to regulate the historical–artistic heritage. It provided a legal concept for excavation and antiquities, stipulated that an inventory of monumental ruins should be created, restricted excavations of private property to the state as well as any incidentally discovered antiquities, empowered the state to authorize excavations, granted ownership of objects discovered to the authors of authorized excavations unless they were nonnationals (for whom access was made difficult, if not actually prohibited), legalized the exchange of antiquities predating the existence of the law and permitted copies of finds to be made for provincial and local museums. Considered as a whole, it was an acceptable law for its time that enabled excavation work to be organized but did not put an end to the problems associated with the ownership of finds. In addition to these technical weaknesses it was also criticized by conservatives during the course of a parliamentary debate, who objected to the control over the circulation of assets and the appropriation by the state of all finds. The law, as previously noted, was supplemented by the provisional regulations governing its implementation, which added a precise time limit for the classification of antiquities (up to the reign of Carlos I) and gave more precise instructions for dealing with issues of exploitation, with the inspector general for fine arts responsible for both areas. The legislation also contained detailed provisions for the creation of a *Junta Superior de Excavaciones y Antigüedades* and special delegates for excavations. Following this, the junta was responsible for issuing permits for excavations and for receiving the records of work. It was also responsible for creating the heritage inventory, produced by its own staff, thus assuming many of the duties previously assigned to the *Comisiones Provinciales de Monumentos,* or Provincial Monuments Commissions (Yáñez 1997; Remesal et al. 2000, p. 26).[6] It therefore became imperative to reform the 1865 Regulations governing the Monuments Commissions. In fact, the new Regulations were approved by the Royal Decree of 11th August 1918 and remained in place until the Provincial Monuments Commissions were finally abolished in 1985 (Almagro 2003, p. 189).

After the new law came into effect in Spain, a relative professionalization in the field of history ensued, both in terms of the individuals associated with official institutions (the *Academia, Escuela Diplomática,* and the universities) and those who had led the drive for improvements from outside, such as the *Institución Libre de Enseñanza.* Even so, between 1912 and 1933 the number of professional archaeologists carrying out excavation work only rose from 39 to 100 (Díaz-Andreu 1997, p. 408).

Emerging within an historical framework that was defined, among other aspects, by the celebration of values such as patriotism, the 1911 law considered that all antiquities discovered by chance underground or during the demolition of old buildings, were the property of the state. It also stipulated that only Spanish researchers authorized by the state could claim ownership of any items found during the course of their excavation work (Article 15) and that foreigners authorized by the state could only own one example of any items they discovered (Article 19) (Yáñez 1997; Farrujia 2004, p. 528).

Once it came into effect, the 1911 Law was quickly implemented in the Canary Islands, specifically in Tenerife, as a result of the Hooton affair (see Farrujia 2010, Chap. 5),[7] but failed to put an end to the plundering of the archaeological heritage of the Canary Islands, which continued to suffer significant losses during the time of the Provincial Archaeological Excavation Commissions (1941–1968) and which is discussed in the next chapter.

---

[6] Following the establishment of the II Republic, the Law on Artistic Heritage was passed on May 13th,1933, replacing the Monuments Commissions with Arts Heritage Boards. After the Civil War, the Commissions were reinstated and reorganized under Decree 3194/1970 as "Historical-Artistic Heritage Commissions." With the establishment of the autonomous communities and the cultural transfers, the "Historical Heritage Commissions" were formed, governed by the Law on Historical Heritage of 16/1985 (Remesal et al. 2000, p. 27).

[7] The North American anthropologist Earnest Albert Hooton (1887–1954) was involved in archaeological excavations in Tenerife in 1915 without authorization under the terms of the 1911 Law. This led to the intervention of the Civil Guard who, nevertheless, failed to seize the indigenous anthropological remains, which found their way to the Peabody Museum at Harvard University in the United States.

References

Almagro Gorbea, M. (2003). *250 años de Arqueología y Patrimonio histórico. Real Academia de la Historia.* Madrid: *Ministerio de Ciencia y Tecnología.* Dirección General de Investigación. Consejería de Educación de la Comunidad de Madrid.

Arco Aguilar, M. C. (1977). El enterramiento Canario Prehispánico. In A. Millares Torres (Eds.), *Historia General de las Islas Canarias* (Vol. I, pp. 311–322). Santa Cruz de Tenerife (Spain): Edirca.

Arco Aguilar, M. C. (1992–1993). De nuevo, el enterramiento canario prehispánico. *Tabona, VIII-I,* 59–75.

Ayarzagüena Sanz, M. (2004). El nacimiento de la Arqueología científica en España. In M. Ayarzagüena Sanz & G. Mora Rodríguez (Eds.), *Pioneros de la Arqueología en España. Del siglo XVI a 1912* (pp. 75–78). Alcalá de Henares: Museo Arqueológico Regional de Madrid.

Bethencourt Alfonso, J. (1902 [1991]). *Historia del pueblo guanche.* Santa Cruz de Tenerife: Lemus.

Blanckaert, C. (2001). Les usages de l'Anthropologie. In C. Blanckaert (Ed.), *Les politiques de l'Anthropologie. Discours et pratiques en France (1860–1940). Histoire des Sciences Humaines* (pp. 9–26). Paris: L'Harmattan.

Cabrera Pérez, J. C. (1996). *La Prehistoria de Fuerteventura: un modelo insular de adaptación.* Madrid: Ediciones del Cabildo Insular de Gran Canaria. Cabildo Insular de Fuerteventura.

Chil y Naranjo, G. (1876). *Estudios históricos, climatológicos y patológicos de las Islas Canarias* (Vol. I). D. Las Palmas de Gran Canaria (Spain): Isidro Miranda Impresor-Editor.

Chil y Naranjo, G. (1886). *Reglamento conforme al cual habrán de llevarse a efecto las exploraciones y rebuscas que se acuerden por la Junta Directiva de El Museo Canario.* Las Palmas de Gran Canaria (Spain): Tipografía La Atlántida.

Coye, N. (2004). La Préhistoire, une science utile. In J. Évin (Ed.), *La Préhistoire en France. 100 ans de découvertes,* (pp. 4–6). Dossiers d'Archeologie, 296. Dijon: Publications de l'Academie.

Díaz-Andreu, M. (1997). Nación e internacionalización. La Arqueología en España en las tres primeras décadas del siglo XX. In G. Mora & M. Díaz-Andreu (Eds.), *La cristalización del pasado: génesis y desarrollo del marco institucional de la Arqueología en España. Actas del II Congreso Internacional de Historiografía de la Arqueología en España* (pp. XVIII–XX), (pp. 403–416). Málaga: Servicio de Publicaciones de la Universidad de Málaga. Ministerio de Educación y Ciencia

Diego Cuscoy, L. (1953). *Nuevas excavaciones arqueológicas en las Canarias Occidentales. Yacimientos de Tenerife y La Gomera (1947–1951). Informes y Memorias de la Comisaría General de Excavaciones Arqueológicas* (Vol. 28). Madrid: Comisaría General de Excavaciones. Ministerio de Educación Nacional.

Diego Cuscoy, L. (1982). El Museo Canario y factores determinantes de su continuidad. *El Museo Canario, XLII,* 7–18.

Farrujia de la Rosa, A. J. (2002). *El poblamiento humano de Canarias en la obra de Manuel de Ossuna y Van den Heede. La Piedra de Anaga y su inserción en las tendencias ideográficas sobre la primera colonización insular. Estudios Prehispánicos, 12.* Madrid: Dirección General de Patrimonio Histórico. Viceconsejería de Cultura y Deportes. Gobierno de Canarias.

Farrujia de la Rosa, A. J. (2004). *Ab Initio (1342–1969). Análisis historiográfico y arqueológico del primitivo poblamiento de Canarias.* Col. Árbol de la Ciencia (Vol. 2). Sevilla: Artemisa Ediciones.

Farrujia de la Rosa, A. J. (2005). *Imperialist archaeology in the Canary Islands. French and German studies on prehistoric colonization at the end of the 19th century. British Archaeological Reports. International Series, 1333.* Oxford: Archaeopress.

Farrujia de la Rosa, A. J. (2009). A history of research into Canarian rock art: opening up new thoughts. *Oxford Journal of Archaeology, 28*(3), 211–226 (August).

Farrujia de la Rosa, A. J. (2010). *En busca del pasado guanche. Historia de la Arqueología en Canarias (1868–1968). Preface by Alain Schnapp.* Santa Cruz de Tenerife (Spain): Edicion Ka.

Gran-Aymerich, E. (2001). *El nacimiento de la Arqueología moderna, 1798–1945 (Naissance de l'archéologie moderne, 1798–1945)*. Zaragoza: Prensas Universitarias de Zaragoza.

Johnson, M. (2000). *Teoría arqueológica. Una introducción (Archaeological theory. An introduction). Colección Ariel Historia*. Barcelona: Editorial Ariel.

Lull, V., & Micó, R. (1997). *Teoría arqueológica I. Los enfoques tradicionales: las arqueologías evolucionistas e histórico-culturales. Revista d'Arqueologia de Ponent, 7,* 107–128.

Maier Allende, J. (2003). Los inicios de la prehistoria en España. Ciencia versus religión. In J. Beltrán Fortes & M. Belén Deamos (Eds.), *El Clero y la Arqueología española. II Reunión Andaluza de Historiografía Arqueológica* (pp. 99–112). Sevilla: Universidad de Sevilla. Fundación El Monte.

Mederos Martín, A. (2003). Islas Canarias. In M. Almagro Gorbea & J. Maier (Eds.), *250 años de Arqueología y Patrimonio* (pp. 195–207). Madrid: Real Academia de la Historia.

Millares, T., A. (1977 [1893]). *Historia General de las Islas Canarias* (Vol. I). Santa Cruz de Tenerife (Spain): Edirca.

Millares Torres, A. (1901). Donativo de la casa de Vega Grande al Museo Canario. *El Museo Canario, X*(114), 45–49.

Ortiz García, C. (2005). La Sociedad Cosmológica de la isla de La Palma. Localismo y ciencia positiva. In A. Vieira (Ed.), *As Ilhas e a Ciência. História da Ciência e das Técnicas. I Seminario Internacional. Centro de Estudios de Historia do Atlántico* (pp. 207–230). Coimbra (Portugal): Ediciones Técnicas.

Pizarroso y Belmonte, C. (1880). *Los aborígenes de Canarias*. Santa Cruz de Tenerife (Spain): Imprenta Isleña de Francisco C. Hernández

Quatrefages de Bréau, A., & Teodore Hamy, E. (1874). La race de Cro-Magnon dans l'espace et dans le temps. *Bulletins de la Société d'Anthropologie de Paris, IX*(2nd serie), 260–266.

Ramírez Sánchez, M. E. (1997). Un acercamiento historiográfico a los orígenes de la investigación arqueológica en Canarias: las Sociedades Científicas del siglo XIX. In G. Mora & M. Díaz-Andreu (Eds.), *La cristalización del pasado: génesis y desarrollo del marco institucional de la Arqueología en España. Actas del II Congreso Internacional de Historiografía de la Arqueología en España* (pp. XVIII–XX), (pp. 311–319). Málaga: Servicio de Publicaciones de la Universidad de Málaga. Ministerio de Educación y Ciencia.

Reglamento. (1878). *Reglamento del Gabinete Científico de Santa Cruz de Tenerife*. Santa Cruz de Tenerife (Spain): Imprenta de Manuel Álvarez.

Reglamento. (1879). *Reglamento de la Sociedad El Museo Canario*. Las Palmas de Gran Canaria: Imprenta de la Atlántida.

Reglamento de la Sociedad Cosmológica de Santa Cruz de La Palma. (2005 [1881]). *Facsimile edition*. Santa Cruz de La Palma: Sociedad Cosmológica de Santa Cruz de La Palma.

Remesal, J., Aguilera, A., & Pons LL (2000). *Comisión de Antigüedades de la Real Academia de la Historia. Cataluña. Catálogo e índices*. Madrid: Real Academia de la Historia. Universitat de Barcelona. Generalitat de Catalunya.

Schnapp, A. (2002). Between antiquarians and archaeologists: Continuities and ruptures. *Antiquity, 76*(291), 134–140.

Trigger, B. (2006). *A history of archaeological thought* (2nd ed.). Cambridge: Cambridge University Press.

Yáñez Vega, A. (1997). Estudio sobre la Ley de Excavaciones y Antigüedades de 1911 y el reglamento para su aplicación de 1912. In G. Mora & M. Díaz-Andreu (Eds.), *La cristalización del pasado: génesis y desarrollo del marco institucional de la Arqueología en España. Actas del II Congreso Internacional de Historiografía de la Arqueología en España* (pp. XVIII–XX), (pp. 423–429). Málaga: Servicio de publicaciones de la Universidad de Málaga. Ministerio de Educación y Ciencia.

Chapter 3
Archaeology and Dictatorship: The Centralization of Archaeological Heritage Management (1939–1975)

The archaeology developed in the Canary Islands at the beginning of the twentieth century underwent a series of important changes that were crucial to its emergence as a scientific discipline. Many of these changes were the result of the path taken by archaeology in the country following the establishment of the Franco regime, with all the administrative reorganization that this entailed, which had significant consequences for archaeological heritage management. However, as in the rest of national territory, Canarian archaeology remained anchored in a fieldwork methodology that was still based on nineteenth-century methods. At the same time, it was clearly influenced by the nationalist discourse of the regime. In addition to historiographical work, archaeological evidence, understood as the "spirit" of the nation, was seen as a keystone in the search for national identity and, together with racial arguments, was used to demonstrate the existence of national unity since time immemorial.

However, the early years of the twentieth century, until around the 1940s, represented a period of crisis in archaeological and anthropological research. Research and publications declined and, in general, the small amount of work that was undertaken was based on information produced by the previous generation. The situation began to change at the end of this period, following the establishment in the Canary Islands of the Provincial Archaeological Excavation Commissions in 1941 (one in the province of Santa Cruz de Tenerife and another in Las Palmas de Gran Canaria). This was the result of the development of the Franco regime or, in other words, a form of politics defined by an authoritarian, unitarian, and ultranationalist state supported by an oligarchy whose political maxims included national unity, a centralized administration, the revival of links to the past, and the vigorous and systematic application of unitarian and assimiliationist cultural policies (Fusí 2000, p. 261; Farrujia 2007). In the Canary Islands, this political scenario pre-empted any autonomous alternatives. From an economic point of view, Francoist politics encouraged the development of a phase of national self-sufficiency in which the development of the Canarian economy would clearly be restricted. Following the Civil War a *sui generis* exchange rate policy was introduced which, together with the tacit suppression of

A. J. Farrujia de la Rosa, *An archaeology of the margins,*
SpringerBriefs in Archaeology, DOI 10.1007/978-1-4614-9396-9_3,
© The Author(s) 2014

the free ports, marked a break with the previous free trade policy.[1] Excessive government intervention in economic affairs led to the definitive suspension of the free port
system and the substitution of European capital with capital from the mainland. The
archipelago was therefore forced to seek supplies from the mainland market, which
were much more expensive, at a time when its capital was being drained by the state.
Self-sufficiency, in this sense, limited purchases from foreign markets and favored
a second conquest of the island market by a Hispanic capitalism that had previously
had an insignificant presence due to its inability to compete with the foreign supply.
As a result, the Canary Islands became a Spanish province, both in political and
economic terms (Macías 2001).

During the course of this new political and economic regime there was also a parallel physical repression of many of the leading authors and intellectuals of previous
years, who were forced into exile, resulting in significant setbacks to Spanish cultural
development.[2] In the Canary Islands, as in the rest of the state, Francoist repression
would imply the persecution of all independent intellectual activity and a ban on all
cultural expression that was not developed within the narrow ideological margins
permitted by the regime. Any social and political criticism was simply suppressed
and external censorship or self-censorship prevailed throughout this period. Consequently, in the field of archaeology prehistoric research in the postwar period was
dominated by men with right-wing, reactionary, conservative, and religious ideas,
both on the mainland (see Estévez and Vila 1999, p. 61, and Wulff 2003) and in the
Canary Islands (see Farrujia 2007, and Navarro and Clavijo 2007).

The impact of this social environment on Canarian archaeology ensured its nationalization, while also allowing for a Spanish-biased interpretation of insular prehistory,
strongly influenced by some of the political premises of the system itself such as national unity, the African aspirations of the regime, and its pro-German leanings. With
regard to this reading of Canarian prehistory, which is emphasized in the following
pages, it should be borne in mind that archaeological research was vulnerable to the
ideological pressures of Francoism. The centralist authoritarianism of the Franco
government not only eliminated regional autonomy in terms of administration and
research, but also led to archaeological work being used to support the aspirations of
the regime. Prehistory was therefore used outside the confines of academic circles
to validate nationalist aspirations (Gracia 2009). In relation to this political use of
archaeology during the Franco regime, it should be noted that the Spanish version of
fascism previously formulated by Miguel Primo de Rivera had already defined the
nation not as a geographical, ethnic, and linguistic reality but essentially as an historical unity with a single destiny. Spanish prehistory, defined by different regional

---

[1] Following the introduction of free ports in 1852, the Canary Islands had benefited from a significant
level of openness to the outside world and broad scope to adapt to international exchange rates. In
this sense, the islands were a political but not an economic Spanish province.

[2] Although in terns of Canarian archaeology it is not possible to refer to exiled archaeologists during
this period, the situation was not the same on the mainland, as can be seen in the cases of Pere Bosch
Gimpera (1891–1974), who left the University of Barcelona and Spain itself, and José Miguel de
Barandiarán Ayerbe (1889–1991), who settled in the northern Basque region until the 1950s.

cultures, therefore fell outside the sphere of national unity propaganda (Corbí 2009). In other words, after the Spanish Civil War, as Díaz-Andreu (1993, p. 82), Ruiz Zapatero (1998, p. 147), and Ortiz García (1998, p. 172) have noted, any non-Spanish, regional approach was crushed and this perspective vanished from historical studies. Francoism also legitimized authoritarianism, referring to religious unity, which had been fought for in the Middle Ages and had resulted in the expulsion of the Moors and the Jews, and the theoretical unification of Spain under the Catholic kings in the fifteenth century, Spain's imperialist past, and even the supposed national unity during the Visigoth period (Díaz-Andreu 1993, p. 74; Wulff 2003, p. 253). Also, during Franco's regime, a number of scholars found the Celt–Iberian theory (based on the Celtic–Iberian origin of Spain) useful to build up a link with the origins of the then rising National Socialism. Franco's nationalism replaced the Iberians with the Celts, promoting the notion that the Iberians were in fact Celts with strong Mediterranean influence (Ruiz et al. 2002).

3.1 Archaeological Heritage Management During the Franco Period

The Francoist administrative policy led to a centralized bureaucracy and this reorganization had direct consequences in the form of the Supreme Council for Scientific Research, founded in 1939, and the creation, by Ministerial Order of March 9th of the same year, of the General Commission for Archaeological Excavations, designed to:

a. Ensure administrative and technical supervision and a scientific basis for future archaeological excavations.
b. Find a solution, through the so-called National Plan, for archaeological problems that had not been investigated by the state.

With the founding of the commission, studies and excavations began in the Canary Islands, Morocco, the Sahara, and Guinea. The Commission, organized by active members of the Falange, replaced the Excavations Department of the Higher Arts Heritage Board which had been operating since 1933, and was organized as a network divided into Provincial, Insular, and Local Commissions. However, the local and provincial network operated beyond the reach of most of the university professors and professionals based in museums. In 1948, during the *II Congreso del Sudeste Espaol* held in Elche, questions would, in fact, be raised about the system due to the lack of professionalism of its staff (Quero 2002, p. 177).

This new administrative approach also favored the concentration of power in the hands of a few individuals who were loyal to the regime, such as Julio Martínez Santa-Olalla (1905–1972), who was appointed General Commissioner (Díaz-Andreu 1993, p. 76).

In the Canary Islands, this centralist administrative policy became effective following the establishment of the Provincial Archaeological Excavation Commissions which were created by the Ministry of Education through the Directorate-General of Fine Arts, under Ministerial Order of 30th April 1941, and were answerable to the General Commission. In the province of Las Palmas de Gran Canaria (comprising Gran Canaria, Lanzarote, and Fuerteventura), Sebastián Jiménez Sánchez (1904–1983) was appointed provincial commissioner and remained in office until 1969, when he resigned. In Santa Cruz de Tenerife (comprising Tenerife, El Hierro, La Gomera, and La Palma), the provincial commissioner was Dacio V. Darias Padrón (1880–1960), who held office from May 14th, 1941 to December 1st, 1942. He was succeeded by the philologist Juan Álvarez Delgado (1900–1987), who served until July 19th, 1951 when he resigned and was replaced by Luis Diego Cuscoy (1907–1987), a member of his team who had been the North Tenerife Local Commissioner since 1948 (Farrujia 2007) [3].

Within this context, Julio Martínez Santa-Olalla was a key figure in the islands due to his influence on Canarian archaeology, supervision of Jiménez Sánchez and Diego Cuscoy, and development of a nationalist discourse that favored a Spanish bias to Canarian prehistory.

Following the establishment of the Provincial Commissions, specifically under the terms of the Decree of 2nd December 1955, the General Commission became known as the National Office for Archaeological Excavations, answerable, as before, to the Directorate-General of Fine Arts and controlled by Julio Martínez Santa-Olalla. The Provincial Commissions were, in turn, replaced by Regional Delegations. In the case of the Canary Islands, because delegations were dependant on a university, the delegation was named the University of La Laguna Regional Delegation. The delegation had to be headed by a university professor working in a field related to archaeological excavation, and Elías Serra Ráfols (1898–1968) was therefore appointed Regional Delegate.[4] Serra's good relations with Diego Cuscoy and Jiménez Sánchez ensured that both remained in office, this time as Provincial Delegates. In Cuscoy's case, his resignation as Provincial Delegate was ratified by Ministerial Order of 24th February 1969, following the establishment in 1968 of the General Inspectorate for Archaeological Excavations covering the whole of Spain and attached to the Board of the National Archaeological Museum of Madrid. Jiménez Sánchez, as previously noted, would also resign in the same year.

The development of this administrative framework, which began in the Canary Islands with the introduction of the Provincial Commissions, presumed the nationalization or Spanish identity of Canarian archaeology, which had not been linked to national research (developed by Spanish archaeologists from the mainland) prior to this and had been strongly influenced by the approach of French authors such as Sabin Berthelot and René Verneau. In addition, the work of the commissions

---

[3] None of these authors were trained archaeologists. For example, Jiménez Sánchez and Diego Cuscoy, two of the most prolific writers, were teachers.

[4] Elías Serra was appointed Professor of Spanish History at the University oif La Laguna on February 22nd, 1926. Subsequently, due to a shortage of staff in the Faculty of Philosophy and Letters, he was also responsible for other courses, including General Cultural History, Universal History, History of Classical Antiquity, and Portuguese Literature.

allowed for a greater understanding of the archaeology of the islands, especially in islands such as Gran Canaria, Tenerife, and La Palma where more fieldwork was undertaken. However, the commission system ultimately led to the isolation of the leaders, inasmuch as no joint work was undertaken by the commissioners in the two provinces to address some of the main issues in Canarian archaeological research (Farrujia 2007).

3.1.1 Museum Institutions and Heritage Management

On an institutional level, the situation regarding Canarian archaeology was very different in the islands of Gran Canaria and Tenerife, the seats of the two provinces and headquarters of the two archaeological museums in the Canary Islands during the Franco period.

3.1.1.1 El Museo Canario

During the Franco regime the museum continued to function and has survived to the present day. However, things were not easy in the early days of the dictatorship, because Jiménez Sánchez, as Commissioner of the Eastern Province and Secretary of El Museo Canario, had to make use of his friendship with Pérez de Barradas, a member of the organization, to request the continuation and greater operational autonomy for the museum institution. It should be noted, in this respect, that the centralizing policy of the Franco regime, directed from Madrid, was responsible for the disappearance of many institutions and this had a particular impact on regions in the country that had their own nationalist identity. This was the case with the *Servei d'Investigacions Arqueologiques* in Catalonia, the *Centro de Investigaciones Prehistóricas de Álava* in the Basque country, and the prehistory, archaeology and history of art departments in the *Seminario de Estudios Galegos* in Galicia (Díaz-Andreu 1993, p. 76; Estevez and Vila 1999, p. 61).

El Museo Canario would finally become attached to the Supreme Council for Scientific Research in 1944. However, it is worth noting that despite the concern of Jiménez Sánchez to defend the interests of the museum institution he represented, its evident Falangist sympathies would prevent full integration (Fig. 3.1).

3.1.1.2 The Tenerife Archaeological Museum

In the case of Tenerife, as previously noted, after the death of Juan Bethencourt Alfonso, the apathy and lack of ability of its own partners and collaborators led to the decline of the *Gabinete Científico*, whose stocks were eventually added to the Bernabé Rodríguez collection and the Santa Cruz de Tenerife Anthropology and Natural History Museum, founded on December 31st, 1902 by the Santa Cruz de

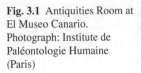

Fig. 3.1 Antiquities Room at
El Museo Canario.
Photograph: Institute de
Paléontologie Humaine
(Paris)

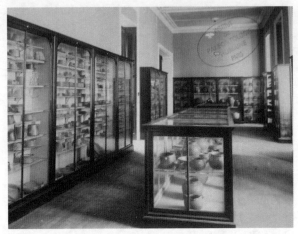

Tenerife City Council. The Tenerife Archaeological Museum was not founded until 1958. The archaeological materials came from fieldwork carried out by the Western Commission, the former Villa Benítez Musem acquired by the Tenerife Council, the Faculty of Philosophy and Letters at the University of La Laguna, private donations, and, above all, the Santa Cruz de Tenerife Natural History Museum. From a thematic point of view, most of the museum focused on the archaeology of Tenerife and a small area was dedicated to indigenous cultures in the rest of the archipelago.

In the case of both the Tenerife Archaeological Museum and El Museo Canario, the only theoretical trend prevailing in the study of Canarian prehistory needless to say was the cultural–historical approach, which is discussed in the next section.

3.2   The "Hispanic" and "Neolithic" Concept of the Indigenous Canarians

In 1934, following the Spanish occupation of the Ifni territory, Martínez Santa-Olalla, in collaboration with the anthropologist José Pérez de Barradas (1897–1981), decided to produce an "Archaeology of the Empire" based on the Hispanic–African prehistoric community, the clearly Spanish nature of the Spanish Sahara (in terms of prehistory, naturally), the whole of Mauritania, and the narrow community between the Canary Islands and the Atlantic (Quero 2002, p. 270).

Within Canarian archaeology, in his approach to the origins of the first settlement on the islands the anthropologist José Pérez de Barradas, who had worked for a period of time in El Museo Canario, argued in 1938 for the existence of a proto-Guanche substratum in the Canary Islands, with clear political implications for outlining the diachronic sequence for the Canarian settlers. The relationship established by Pérez de Barradas between this substratum, the cave cultures, and the Spanish Sahara, enabled him to endorse the nationalist politics of the Franco regime inasmuch as, in

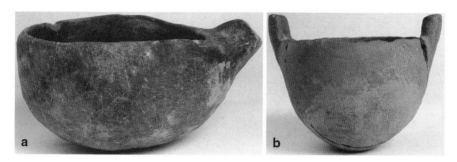

Fig. 3.2 Handmade indigenous ceramics from Tenerife (*Gánigo*), which Francoist archaeologists associated with North African Neolithic ceramics. Photograph: Museo Arqueológico de Tenerife

the final analysis, the first settlers in the Iberian peninsula, the Canary Islands, and the Spanish colony in Africa would have shared the same racial and cultural roots in ancient times (Pérez 1939). Diego Cuscoy and Jiménez Sánchez, influenced by the arguments of Pérez de Barradas, also supported this hypothesis. They therefore defended the common (racial and cultural) origins of the first inhabitants of the Canary Islands, the Iberian peninsula, and the Spanish Sahara, thus reinforcing the idea of national unity since time immemorial and legitimizing the African aspirations of the regime.

From an archaeological point of view, the whole series of supposedly Neolithic features allegedly detected in the examples of indigenous Canarian material culture (ceramics, lithic industry, bone industry, etc.) fit perfectly with the Neolithic-biased vision which at the time, and since the end of the nineteenth century, had been claimed for the first human settlements on the islands. Moreover, all these traits seemed to correspond to those defined for the Ibero–Mauritanian and Ibero–Saharan cultures which were seen as part of the proto-Berber substrate. The Hispano–Mauritanian culture, dating from the third millennium BC, was defined by a polished stone industry, flint knapping, a rudimentary bone industry, and ceramics consisting of plain vessels and elaborately decorated containers, stamped with shell motifs and in many cases also painted. The Ibero–Saharan culture, dating from the beginning of the second half of the third millennium BC, was defined by elaborate flint knapping, keeled and geometric ceramics uniformly painted and sometimes displaying decorative motifs, bone tools, carefully worked cut stone items, and a habitat consisting of well-constructed settlements (Martínez Santa-Olalla 1946; Pericot 1953, p. 271; Fig. 3.2).

Thus the forced comparisons made between the Canarian world and African prehistory ensured that very high chronologies were accepted at the time to establish the early colonization of the islands. It was only by manipulating these chronologies that it became possible to relate the first settlements on the islands to the dates for the North African context. Moreover, as the studies produced by Spanish archaeologists on the mainland claimed that the first Neolithic evidence common to North Africa and the Spanish Levant (the so-called Ibero–Mauritanian region) could not be earlier than the third millennium, this implied that the first settlement of the Canary Islands, to which they attributed the same origins, could not be earlier than this either (Farrujia 2003). Thus, without the aid of absolute dating, the third millennium BC was eventually accepted as the *terminus post quem* or, in other words, as the date before which the islands were uninhabited.

From a racial point of view, defending this hypothesis for the first settlement of the Canary Islands implied that the Cro-Magnon type present in the Archipelago could have been related to the ethnic base of the Oranian culture in northeastern Africa, derived from the Mechta-el-Arbi and Afalou-bu-Rhummel race, which supposedly arrived on the islands during their Neolithic period (Pericot 1953, p. 273). It should be noted that the so-called Mechta–Afalou type, based on the Algerian sites of Mechta el Arbi and Afalou bou Rhummel, had already been defined by Henri Victor Vallois in 1934 as a result of discoveries made in the 1920s. Subsequently, close similarities were found with the French Cro-Magnon type (a craniofacial imbalance, rectangular-shaped eye sockets, height, etc.) and these studies were aided by the large quantity of bone remains found (amounting to almost 500), three-quarters of which appeared to be associated with the Ibero–Mauritanian industry, nowadays dated at between 22,000 and 8,000 BP. (Fernández 2001, p. 170). [5]

Thus, whereas for nineteenth-century evolutionist scholars the center of origin for the Cro-Magnon race was France, a location that enabled them to incorporate the Guanche within universal history, for the Francoists it was North Africa and was associated with the area occupied by the then-Spanish colonies and originally by the Ibero–Mauritanian and Ibero–Saharan cultures. This concept provided a definitive argument for Spanish national unity since early times.

In the Canary Islands therefore, the concept of prehistory imposed by the leading authorities was combined with the concept of the unified destiny (in a universal sense) of Spain, religious anticommunism, and links with the Berber or Amazigh world. The connection between the Canary Islands and the Berbers was accepted by the Francoist scientific community, among other reasons because it implied a link between the Canary Islands and white Africa. Due to racial prejudice, any links with black, Sub-Saharan Africa were ignored. Also, the Paleo-Berbers were considered responsible for the Ibero–Mauritanian and Ibero–Saharan cultures (Hachid 2000; Maddy-Weitzman 2012).

Cultural historicism provided the theoretical framework for this analysis. The ideology of the Francoist authors was responsible for ensuring the success of the theory of the great cultural circles, because the belief that there was a Lower Palaeolithic era that extended throughout the world with remarkable uniformity and therefore a uniform mentality in early humanity, came from the Catholic and extremely conservative anthropology of those years. The Catholic priests Hugo Obermaier (German)

---

[5] Desanges (1983) notes that it is unlikely that this race would have reached the Canary Islands, because although the Guanche appear to belong to the Mechta-el-Arbi racial type in anthropological terms, there are no links with their industry and customs. Desanges also questions the validity of the term Ibero–Mauritanian, because archaeology has shown that this civilization could not have come from Europe.

Fig. 3.3 Tomb in Gáldar (Gran Canaria), which Francoist archaeologists associated with tombs documented in the Spanish Sahara. Photograph: El Museo Canario

and Henri Breuil (French) were, from the moment they arrived in Spain at the beginning of the twentieth century, the key figures in the construction of the Spanish Paleolithic. This was due as much to the importance of their work as to the influence that their proposals and they themselves had on the Spanish archaeologists who were working on the subject at that time. They arrived at just the right moment because, even though Spanish authors were well informed about the work that was taking place in other parts of Europe, the arrival of these two wise foreigners (of a clearly orthodox persuasion) added impetus to the systematization of the different activities that were being carried out at the time and to the organization of the evidence that was being discovered (Vila and Estévez 2010) (Fig. 3.3).

From this cultural–historical perspective, the intention was to define archaeological cultures spatially, chronologically, and culturally from a series of similar characteristics based on a sufficiently broad set of examples of material culture (such as ceramics, burial typologies, and plans of houses) and to understand cultural (and therefore historical) change through diffusion or, alternatively, the replacement of settlements. In this sense the Francoist authors, loyal to the ideas of the creators of cultural circles, explained the cultural similarities between the Canary Islands and other spheres of reference as either the result of a common ethnic substrate or intensive trading relations. The cultural convergence concept of the evolutionists did not fit into these arguments, although it is clear that some authors, such as Pérez de Barradas, tried to establish an evolutionary sequence for Canarian Neolithic culture from a techno-morphological point of view, basically by resorting to the study of ceramics. Nevertheless cultural historicism, based on diffusionism, remained the theoretical model.

This Spanish-biased concept of the indigenous Canarian population was accompanied by the coining of a new term, *pre-Hispanic*, to designate the historical period extending from the first settlement on the Canary Islands to their annexation by the Crown of Castile. The term was introduced into the Canarian context by Julio Martínez Santa-Olalla and, in fact, implied an entire ideological baggage, because it reinforced the link between the Canary Islands and Spanish national identity, while annulling the preceding cultural identity, which was explained purely by the Hispanic argument. With the term pre-Hispanic, the indigenous culture that had existed prior to the conquest and colonization of the islands simply became pre-Hispanic, predating the civilizing effect of the Spanish. The actual Canarian culture, and therefore the North African culture of the primitive islanders (of Amazigh origins), was undervalued and acquired meaning only in terms of a Spanish frame of reference.

References

Corbí, J. M. (2009). El franquismo en la arqueología: el pasado prehistórico y antiguo para la España una, grande y libre. Arqueoweb. Revista sobre arqueología en internet. http://www.pendientedemigracion.ucm.es/info/arqueoweb/pdf/11/corbi.pdf. Accessed 11 Jan 2011.

Díaz-Andreu, M. (1993). Theory and ideology in archaeology: Spanish archaeology under the Franco régime. *Antiquity, 67,* 74–82.

Estévez, J., & Vila, A. (1999). *Piedra a Piedra. Historia de la construcción del Paleolítico en la Península Ibérica. BAR Internacional Series, 805.* Oxford: Archaeopress.

Farrujia de la Rosa, A. J. (2003). The Canary Islands under Franco's dictatorship: Archaeology, national unity and African aspirations. *Journal of Iberian Archaeology, 5,* 209–222.

Farrujia de la Rosa, A. J. (2007). *Arqueología y franquismo en Canarias. Política, poblamiento e identidad (1939–1969). Colección Canarias Arqueológica* (Vol. 2). Santa Cruz de Tenerife (Spain): Organismo Autónomo de Museos y Centros. Cabildo de Tenerife

Fernández Martínez, V. (2001). La idea de África en el origen de la prehistoria española: una perspectiva postcolonial. *Complutum, 12,* 167–184.

Fusí Aizpurúa, J. P. (2000). *España. La evolución de la identidad nacional.* Madrid: Ediciones Temas de Hoy.

Gracia Alonso, F. (2009). *La Arqueología durante el primer franquismo (1939–1956).* Barcelona: Ediciones Bellaterra.

Hachid, M. (2000). *Les premiers berberes: entre Mediterranee, Tassili et Nil.* Aix-en-Provence: Edisud.

Macías Hernández, A. M. (2001). Canarias: una economía insular y atlántica. In L. Germán, E. Llopis,J. Maluquer de Motes & S. Zapata (Eds.), *Historia Económica Regional de España. Siglos XIX y XX,* (pp. 476–506). Barcelona: Editorial Crítica.

Maddy-Weitzman, B. (2012). *The Berber identity movement and the challenge to North African States.* Austin: University of Texas Press.

Martínez Santa-Olalla, J. (1946). *Esquema paletnológico de la Península Hispánica* (2nd ed.). Madrid: Publicaciones del Seminario de Historia Primitiva del Hombre.

Navarro Mederos, J. F., & Clavijo Redondo, M. A. (2007). Africanismos y atlantismos. La Arqueología en la isla de La Palma durante el periodo franquista. *Tabona, 16,* 133–166.

Ortiz García, C. (1998). Folklore y Franquismo. In R. Huertas, & C. Ortiz García (Eds.), *Ciencia y fascismo* (pp. 162–179). Madrid: Ediciones Doce Calles.

Pérez de Barradas, J. (1939). *Estado actual de las investigaciones prehistóricas sobre Canarias. Memoria acerca de los estudios realizados en 1938 en "El Museo Canario".* Las Palmas de Gran Canaria (Spain): Publicaciones de El Museo Canario.

Pericot García, L. (1953). Historia de Marruecos, I. Prehistoria. Primera Parte. El Paleolítico y Epipaleolítico. Tetuán (Morocco): Instituto General Franco de Estudios e Investigación Hispano-árabe. Editora Marroquí

Quero Castro, S. (2002). La investigación del Paleolítico en Madrid durante el franquismo (1936–1971). In J. Panera Gallego & S. Rubio Jara (Eds.), *Bifaces y Elefantes. La investigación del Paleolítico Inferior en Madrid. Revista Zona Arqueológica, 1* (pp. 169–193). Madrid: Museo Arqueológico Regional.

Ruiz, A., Sánchez, A., & Bellón, J. P. (2002). The History of Iberian Archaeology: one archaeology for two Spains. *Antiquity, 76,* 184–190.

Ruiz Zapatero, G. (1998). La distorsión totalitaria: las "raíces prehistóricas" de la España franquista. In R. Huertas, & C. Ortiz García (Eds.), *Ciencia y fascismo* (pp. 147–159). Madrid: Ediciones Doce Calles.

Vila, A., & Estévez, J. (2010). Obermaier and the construction of the Spanish paleolithic: A view from the 21st century. *Mitteilungen der Gesellschaft für Urgeschichte, 19,* 35–50.

Wulff Alonso, F. (2003). *Las esencias patrias. Historiografía e Historia Antigua en la construcción de la identidad espaola (siglos XVI-XX).* Barcelona: Editorial Crítica.

Chapter 4
In Search of the Indigenous Culture of the Canary Islands (1975–2012)

Political, social, economic, and cultural scenarios condition the forms and ways in which historians and archaeologists "appropriate" specific pasts (Wallerstein 2003; Lozny 2011, p. 23), and also the major phases that have marked changes in images of the "Other," the "savage," and prehistory. These scenarios have, in turn, influenced scientific and ideological paradigms (Farrujia 2010; Patou-Mathis 2011). In this sense, as argued in previous chapters, the replacement of each historical conjunction was followed systematically by a change in the way in which historical discourses were constructed. These changes involve the creation of specific versions of the past history of the Canary Islands, all of which are completely different from each other and sometimes totally contradictory, while all tending to justify the social order established in the particular period in which they are produced. Thus the "indigenous Canarian of European origins" from the end of the nineteenth century became the "indigenous Canarian of Hispanic origins" with Ibero–Saharan and Ibero–Mauritanian roots during the Franco period. Parallel to this, archaeological heritage management underwent certain changes that nevertheless failed to improve the organization, understanding, protection, and dissemination of the indigenous heritage. The nineteenth-century private initiatives, represented by museums and offices run by bourgeois Canarian intellectuals, were replaced in the twentieth century by the intervention of the Franco government, involving a centralized management, the development of fieldwork, a greater number of excavations, and the reinforcement of a colonial discourse. Canarian archaeological evidence was analyzed on the basis of this colonialist discourse and this knowledge was essentially disseminated via the museums. The mummies and indigenous artifacts (primarily ceramics and lithic and bone tools) displayed in glass cases and interpreted from this point of view helped reinforce a simplistic "Neolithic" reading of indigenous Canarian societies among the general public. In other words, the Spanish government imposed its particular vision of heritage, set up an institutional framework and organized conservation practices in the Canary Islands. An unequal power relationship was therefore the starting point for any consideration of the Canarian heritage on the part of the Franco regime. The archaeology of the Canary Islands was perceived through the "filter" of the knowledge produced by the "new colonizers" and the prevailing influence of French authors in nineteenth-century research was replaced by the scientific interventionism of authors loyal to the Franco regime.

A. J. Farrujia de la Rosa, *An archaeology of the margins,*
SpringerBriefs in Archaeology, DOI 10.1007/978-1-4614-9396-9_4,
© The Author(s) 2014

The turning point came in 1968 when archaeologists were included in the University of La Laguna for the first time, including the leading figure of Manuel Pellicer Catalán, Professor of Archaeology and Prehistory, who headed the recently created Department of Archaeology, Prehistory and Ethnology. Archaeological research therefore became linked to academic and university work and specialist training.

The department developed the following as research priorities: further excavations in order to obtain examples of material culture, absolute dating, and cultural sequencing using a stratigraphic archaeological method, and plans for the excavation of a sufficient number of sites in each island using stratigraphy in order to produce a comparative stratigraphic study and determine dates for the arrival of the first populations on the islands (Pellicer 1968–1969). Archaeological studies enabled the first settlement on the islands to be dated at around the fifth century BC, meaning that the links established between the Canarian archipelago and the prehistoric Ibero–Mauritanian and Ibero–Saharan cultures could therefore be rejected. This new reading of Canarian archeology coincided with a relaxation of the Franco regime and a crisis in its African mission, in the form of the loss of Equatorial Guinea in 1968. The Spanish Sahara, now Western Sahara, was, in turn, occupied by the Moroccans in 1975 (Farrujia and García 2005). Parallel to this, the scientific community emphasized the need to study the African context in order to deepen the understanding of Canarian archaeology (Farrujia 2003).

However, this new focus, which has been developed up to the present day, has not been accompanied by any revision of theory, because cultural historicism, the great legacy of the dictatorship, has remained the predominant model. In this sense, as Hernández Gómez et al. (2004–2005) and Farrujia (2008, 2011) have noted, many archaeological studies still contain echoes of the ethnocentric, colonial, flat, and simplistic vision of indigenous Canarian societies, despite emphasizing their African roots. As Lozny (2011, p. 28) has pointed out, it seems that nineteenth-century German-devised culture-history is the most common archaeological paradigm around the world and this has contributed to the use of archaeological data for nationalistic purposes, whereas other approaches, such as processual studies or historical ecology, are far less popular. Its popularity might be due to the fact that it answers the most basic questions about the past, such as who, when, and where, but not necessarily how or why.

The archaeology of the Canary Islands therefore shares three of the most common characteristics of social histories of archaeology worldwide, as defined by authors such as Hodder (2001), Trigger (2006), and Lozny (2011): (a) a culture-history approach as the key methodology and basis for locally generated theories (with a strong nationalistic flavor), (b) the use of archaeology for political (nationalistic) goals, and (c) a tendency to relate archaeological research topics to existing political conditions and demands. The next section analyzes the legal framework for the Canarian archaeological heritage in terms of the social, economic, and symbolic importance attributed to it by the authorities.

4.1   The Legal Framework and Archaeological Heritage Management in the Canary Islands

As discussed in the second chapter, it was not until 1911 that the legal vacuum surrounding heritage was remedied with the Law of 7 July on Excavations and An- tiquities, whose Regulations were approved on March 1st, 1912. This law established the legal framework for archaeological excavations in Spain and regulations for the preservation of ruins and antiquities, as well as heritage properties in general (build- ings of artistic interest). The protection of all works of art and products dating from prehistory, antiquity, and the Middle Ages fell within the scope of this law.

The term *heritage,* referring to the collective legacy worth preserving, acquired an administrative and legal meaning not only in Spain but also more generally in the West during the first half of the twentieth century. After the Second World War the concept was extended to an international context and subsequently a number of concepts emerged from the legal world that were associated with heritage and related to the idea of ownership, namely *asset*, *legacy*, and *property* (Harrison 2012, Chap. 3).

This concern on the part of the public authorities with heritage has meant that all expressions and manifestations of art fall within the sphere of law. Moreover, cultural assets are dealt with in law not only in terms of their aesthetic interest but also the social, economic, and symbolic interest attributed to them. Therefore, as Querol Fernández has noted (2010), the legal history of cultural assets parallels the history of law, rather than the history of art. In this sense, as Willems (2012, p. 37) has also pointed out, archaeology is about the past, but archaeological heritage management is about the role of the past in the present. Heritage is perceived as relevant because it contributes towards defining identity and often to the legitimizing of power. Managing archaeological heritage is therefore never neutral and is always politically sensitive to some extent.

After the 1911 law came into force, a whole series of key measures affecting spe- cific aspects of heritage were adopted in Spain, such as the 1931 law on the trading of bibliographical and documentary assets, the 1940 decree on the inventory of mon- uments, and the 1972 law on the protection of the documentary and bibliographical heritage (García 1987).

Faced with this fragmented scenario, Law 16/1985 of 25 June on the Spanish Historical Heritage (hereinafter the LPHE) provided a coherent legal framework. Before turning to some aspects of this law, it should be noted that the 1978 Spanish Constitution structured the country as a state based on autonomous communities (consisting of 17 autonomous communities, or local authorities, including the Canary Islands), each with their own powers, including those relating to culture. In fact, the statutes for the different communities were approved between 1979 and 1984 (in the case of the Canary Islands, on August 10th, 1982).[1] In addition, the Spanish

---

[1] Article 39.9 of the Statutes of Autonomy of the Autonomous Community of the Canary Is- lands marked the exclusive transfer of responsibility for the historical, artistic, archaeological, ethnographic, and paleontological heritage to the Canarian Directorate-General for Historical Heritage.

Constitution covers various aspects associated with the preservation of the Spanish historical heritage and specifies the powers assumed by the state in this area (Art. 44–46) and it was only after the Spanish Constitution became effective that the task of elaborating the LPHE began.

4.1.1 Law 16/1985 of 25 June on the Spanish Historical Heritage

The LPHE establishes a constitutional, heterogeneous, and decentralized legal system whose purpose is to safeguard and foster the material culture produced by human beings in the broadest sense. The law consists of nine main sections, six provisions, and a total of 79 articles. The final provision authorizes the government to establish any regulations it deems necessary and, in fact, given the need for a Regulation on Partial Development, the Royal Decree 111/1986 of 10 January was approved. This had four sections, covering aspects relating to the bodies involved (Title I), the declaration of BICs (*Bienes de Interés Cultural*, Assets of Cultural Interest) and their general register, the General Inventory of Moveable Property (Title II), exports, licensing, and the like (Title III) and promotion measures (Title IV).

The main contributions and features of the Law and Decree on Heritage are:

- *The concept of historical heritage*: The LPHE introduces a new concept of historical heritage based on extrajudicial criteria such as artistic, historical, and archaeological interest (Art. 1), combined with cultural assets, which are divided into movable and immovable properties. Within the category of immovable property various types of assets can be defined and declared BICs (monuments, historical gardens, areas, and sites and archaeological zones). The cultural assets category also includes four special types of heritage: archaeological; ethnographic; documentary and bibliographic; and archives, libraries, and museums.

  It is important to establish that what is considered an archaeological asset in Spain (whose study and knowledge requires the application of an archaeological methodology) does not correspond to the legal definition in other countries, in which archaeological heritage is considered to be restricted to a particular age limit (e.g., 100 years in Puerto Rico), a definite period in history, such as the pre-Hispanic period (Costa Rica and Mexico), or has a particular scientific or cultural significance (Cuba) (Mestre 2012). In a general sense, in most of the European countries, archaeological heritage is considered as the legacy of physical artifacts (such as buildings, monuments, landscapes, and artifacts) that are inherited from past generations, maintained in the present, and bestowed for the benefit of future generations (Willems 1998, 2010).

  The LPHE also establishes a distinction between historical and natural heritage, because the former is the result of human action, in its broadest sense, and consists of movable and immovable property of a particular type (archaeological, ethnographic, museum, archive, and library), as well as intangible assets such as dance, music, and customs.

- *Historical units*: Defined in the LPHE as immovable cultural assets, consisting of settlement units that reflect the evolution of a human community or are evidence of its culture. Only units that have been declared BICs can be classified as protected and there can be no general rehabilitation work in cities in areas bordering on these units. The conservation measures envisaged in the LPHE include preserving the urban and architectural structure, urban remodeling, and cataloguing units for the purposes of legal protection.
- *The social value of the historical heritage*: The LPHE emphasizes the social value of the historical heritage, providing citizens with access to cultural assets.
- *Levels of protection for the historical heritage*: There are three categories: (a) undeclared cultural assets, protected under National Information Plans; (b) registered and declared cultural assets, namely movable properties, included in the General Inventory of Moveable Property; and (c) BICs, the major category of protected assets, included in the General Register of Assets of Cultural Interest and depending on state administration. The BIC category implies that items benefit from special state supervision in terms of their conservation and protection.
- *Protection measures for BICs*: A ban on their displacement or removal, unless necessary; a ban on any unauthorized building work, and so on. The law also defines all the administrative measures that may be used by the state authorities to protect and enhance heritage, such as policing (of archaeological excavations or exports); inspections and inventories; promotional measures; and coercive measures in the form of sanctions, penalties, and restrictions on ownership, among others.
- *Principles of conservation and restoration*: The law establishes that the state authorities must adopt specific measures to conserve, consolidate, and improve BICs.
- *Autonomous communities*: The LPHE begins by considering the division of powers between the state and the autonomous communities. It establishes that the communities are responsible for the assets that form part of their heritage, whereas those associated with public services managed by the state or included in the national heritage are the responsibility of the state. The autonomous communities are also responsible for crafts, museums, libraries, and music conservatories of interest to the community, promoting culture and research and, where applicable, the teaching of the community language. The LPHE further stipulates that the state is responsible for attributing the status of BIC (a point that was later changed, as we show in the next section) and the protection of cultural assets with regard to illegal exportation and spoliation.

4.1.2 The Powers of the Autonomous Communities and Law 4/1999 of 15 March on the Historical Heritage of the Canary Islands

After the LPHE came into effect, the division of responsibilities between the state and the autonomous communities became one of the most controversial areas. The sticking point involved the authority attributed to the state to declare BIC status, which the autonomous communities considered an invasion of their powers. Royal Decree 64/1994, modifying Royal Decree 111/1986, introduced certain changes, including:

- Dissemination of the historical heritage on an international basis to be shared by the state and the autonomous communities, provided that this did not economically or politically compromise the central administration.
- Declarations of BIC status by royal decree (a procedure exclusive to the state) only required for state BICs. The autonomous communities may declare their own properties BIC without the intervention of the central administration.
- The autonomous communities to be responsible for intervening in the case of spoliation, whereas the state could act in accordance with the principle of minimum intervention.

All changes to the LPHE were obviously reflected in Law 4/1999 of 15 March on the Historical Heritage of the Canary Islands, as well as in laws pertaining to other autonomous communities who issued their own legislation, as in the case of Castile–La Mancha (1990), the Basque Country (1990), Andalusia (1991), Catalonia (1993), and Galicia (1995). In fact, almost all powers pertaining to heritage are nowadays invested in the autonomous communities, with only a small margin reserved for the central administration, and the role of the municipalities is more restricted than it should be. In this regard, Spain operates almost as a federal state (Querol and Castillo 2012).

In the specific case of the Canary Islands and from a legal point of view, the approach to the archaeological heritage in Law 4/1999 is based on continuity, because it develops what had been established in the 1911 Law on Excavations and Antiquities and subsequently reiterated in the LPHE. In this sense, it emphasizes public ownership of all archaeological items, covers documentation in the form of archaeological maps, and presents a series of legal instruments to prevent the destruction of historical heritage assets. Within this continuity, the innovation introduced by Law 4/1999 involves the regulation of archaeological parks (Art. 63), defining them as areas containing BIC sites categorized as archaeological zones, which are open to the public (open public spaces).

From the point of view of heritage management, Article 8 of Law 4/1999 establishes that the councils of each island are responsible for the conservation and administration of the island historical heritage.[2] They are also obliged to produce the relevant information required for preparing Special Protection Plans for Historical Units, Archaeological Zones, and Historical Sites and for processing BIC declarations, which they must submit to the government of the Canary Islands for approval. The councils are also responsible for planning and implementing policies for museums and archaeological parks of interest to the islands.

---

[2] The Island Council is a modern administrative body exclusive to the Canary Islands, whose origins lie in the councils or governing boards of the old regime. They are the administrative bodies that exist on each of the islands in the archipelago (El Hierro, La Gomera, La Palma, Tenerife, Gran Canaria, Lanzarote, and Fuerteventura).

However, all these legal protection measures are very bureaucratic: the assets are declared and catalogued or, in other words, established on paper or in files. Moreover, the majority of protection measures, in practical terms, have no impact on conservation. In this sense, the status of Archaeological Zone does not imply putting an end to spoliation which, unfortunately, is very common in Canarian sites (Farrujia 2012). The following section analyzes the exact nature of Canarian archaeological assets in relation to the immediate Spanish context and explores certain questions associated with their place within the international heritage context.

4.2   The Nature of Canarian Archaeological Assets in the Colonial Era

The colonial past of the Canary Islands has had a clear influence on the development and evolution of Canarian archaeology, as shown in previous chapters. This framework has, in turn, shaped archaeological heritage management in the islands. Consequently, the study of the interrelations between the colonial past and Canarian archaeological studies may be considered relevant to the subject of archaeology in an international context for three reasons. First of all, it provides an almost unique opportunity for uncovering the history of archaeology within the margins of Europe (in fact, in an African region) and exploring colonial and foreign influences. In many ways it is a mirror of archaeological mainstreams and an exercise in (re)thinking the aim and status of present-day archaeology.

Secondly, it is an exceptional opportunity for revealing the "weight of tradition" by presenting a form of archaeological heritage management that has interesting oppositions, namely the European/monumental heritage (Castilian monuments and buildings) versus the African/nonmonumental heritage (Amazigh or ancient Canarian sites). In this sense, given the monumental, lavish, and artistic nature of the antiquities of mainland Spain (Iberian, Roman, Visigoth, and Arab, to give just a few examples), the archaeology of the Canary Islands is very different. As argued in the Introduction, the material culture of the indigenous settlements in the archipelago is characterized by greater simplicity and sobriety: handmade ceramic vessels that are sparsely decorated (except in the case of the Gran Canaria ceramics); lithic tools made essentially from obsidian or basalt; the bone industry; very few metal objects; the predominance of cave dwellings, and so on. This explains, to a great extent, why most of the illegal trade in archaeological assets in the Canary Islands from the eighteenth century onwards centered on plundering burial caves, where the much-coveted Guanche mummies could be found, usually disregarding the actual material culture associated with them. There was also a significant plundering of other anthropological material (basically skulls), which also involved foreign researchers who arrived in the islands to study Canarian archaeology.

The third important reason is that the situation in the Canary Islands provides an opportunity to study the role played by colonialism in archaeological heritage management. Modern European colonialism affected the whole world and its legacy is still overwhelming today, as Trigger (2006) and González Ruibal (2010) have argued. From this point of view, it is sufficient to cite the works and thoughts of European archaeologists in other continents. However, since Said's *Orientalism* (1979) we know that colonial categories not only constructed an image of the Other, but also played a fundamental role in shaping European identity, science, and politics and a specific relationship therefore exists between colonialism and European archaeology.

Many books have appeared recently on European archaeological heritage management[3] and several on colonialism and archaeology,[4] but the possibility of researching both aspects within Europe, in the Canary Islands, is certainly an extraordinary phenomenon, even taking the following fact into account: in the Canary Islands there is no indigenous archaeology (i.e., archaeological research and heritage management produced by and for indigenous people) because as previously noted, the conquest and colonization of the Canarian archipelago led to the gradual disappearance of the precolonial societies. However, the European colonial discourse that influenced archaeology in other indigenous contexts (Australia, Africa, etc.) is also evident in the Canary Islands. As Ireland (2010) has pointed out, indigenous and nonindigenous communities are all engaged in the active "use" of the colonial archaeological heritage as much as any other form of tangible or intangible heritage. In this sense, the archaeology developed in the Canary Islands during the nineteenth century was clearly influenced by French colonial policy in North Africa and French imperialist aspirations regarding the Canaries. This led to efforts to relate the first settlements on the islands to French prehistory, the Cro-Magnon race, and "white" populations.

Later, for a large part of the twentieth century and coinciding with the Franco regime, the colonial focus remained intact, although the first inhabitants of the Canary Islands were now linked to the prehistoric "Hispanic" (Ibero–Mauritanian and Ibero–Saharan) culture located, in territorial terms, in the Spanish colonial possessions in North Africa. As this paralleled the consolidation of the nation state during the Franco regime, even (indigenous Canarian) archaeological cultures had to be fully incorporated into the common project in order to support the idea of national unity since prehistoric times. The state's attitude towards the former indigenous Canarian people was often comparable to attitudes in the overseas colonies, although one unsolvable ambiguity remained: the indigenous people were ridiculed as primitive, but at the same time were considered the cultural ancestors of the nation (Farrujia 2003).

This archaeological perspective which still, in the twenty-first century, influences certain aspects of the way in which the indigenous past of the Canary Islands is viewed, was developed even though its historical subject—the indigenous population—did not survive. The social factors involved in Canarian archaeology

---

[3] The works of Cleere (1984 and 2000), Willems (2007), Smith and Waterton (2009), and Mauch and Smith (2010), among others, are illustrative in this respect.

[4] See, for example, the work of Lyons and Papadopoulos (2002) Gosden (2004), Dietler (2010), Burchac, Hart, and Wobs (2010), Carlson and McHalsie (2010), or Lydon and Rizvi (2010), among others.

were Europeans, in particular the Spanish.[5] It may be said that we now have new, postmodern empires without colonies, endowed with their own knowledge–power strategies. In this sense, according to Ireland (2010), the role of heritage has been closely linked to the construction and reinforcement of national and ethnic identities and, in the postcolonial world, to projects that still legitimize colonial occupation. The Canary Islands are not a Spanish colony, but one of the autonomous communities that make up the country. At the same time, however, it is a geographical area politically controlled by a distant country, a vestige of a past empire, a national territory next to the African continent. In other words they are an overseas territory like the French "Départements d'Outre-Mer" or DOM (Guadeloupe, Guyana, Martinique, and Reunion) and are considered an Outermost Region (OMR) by the European Union. The actual geostrategic location of the Canarian archipelago in the Atlantic has helped to reinforce historically the concept of the islands as a Spanish overseas possession and a strategic enclave in relation to the neighboring continent of Africa.[6] These factors and the almost total lack of theory renewal within Canarian archaeology help to explain, to a great extent, why the colonial discourse still lives on in archaeology in the Canary Islands.

In other geographical contexts in which the indigenous populations survived, the colonial discourse proved useful in denying indigenous peoples their roots and historical land rights. Whenever monuments were discovered in "primitive" lands, from sub-Saharan Africa to Australia, they were automatically linked to superior, white populations that had supposedly occupied the land before the arrival of the present inhabitants. This strategy was supported by diffusionist ideas in the early twentieth century, which conceived of a very restricted number of creative core areas from which cultural products spread all over the world (Trigger 2006; González-Ruibal 2010). In this sense, it may be said that the European colonial discourse developed in indigenous environments also affected Canarian archaeology, despite the fact that the indigenous societies did not survive in the archipelago.

Within this scenario, what is the role of postcolonial discourse in Canarian archaeology? Due to limitations of space, the main postcolonial works developed by ethnic

---

[5] The work of the Moroccan linguist Ahmed Sabir (2008), focusing on an analysis of the linguistic and cultural parallels between the Canarian and Moroccan Amazigh environments, is an exception. This is the first publication in which a North African Moroccan researcher has engaged with the study of the indigenous Canarian world. However, Sabir's work is closely tied to Canarian ethnohistorical sources which, as noted in the Introduction, were written by European colonialists and presented an ethnocentric view of the indigenous Canarian past. In addition, the work makes repeated use of concepts that are the result of this colonial legacy within Canarian archaeological discourse (pre-Hispanic, aboriginal, prehistory). The conceptual problematic within Canarian archaeology has been analyzed elsewhere (Farrujia, 2010). Sabir's main contribution lies in contextualizing the cultural evidence of the indigenous Canarian culture in terms of indigenous Canarian words that have been preserved in the sources, using an ethnolinguistic approach. The study highlights the unquestionable Amazigh roots of the indigenous Canarian societies, although the research, in terms of African studies, is restricted to the present-day South Moroccan region.

[6] The geostrategic importance of the Canary Islands has been reassessed since 1975 in light of the tripartite agreement on the Sahara, the Spanish–Moroccan treaties and Spain's entry into the North Atlantic Treaty Organization (NATO) following the referendum held in March 1986.

minorities or subaltern groups at the centers of theory production (Spivak 1985; Chatterjee 1993; Bhabha 1994, among others) are not discussed here. However, it is important to emphasize that postcolonial studies are important to the different configurations of contemporary theorization in archaeology. In fact, there are three distinct areas in which postcolonial studies are linked to archaeology: (a) interpretively, in the investigation of past episodes of colonization and colonialism, using the archaeological record; (b) historically, in the study of the role of archaeology in the construction and deconstruction of colonial discourses; (c) methodologically, as an aid to decolonizing the discipline and as a guide for ethical practices in contemporary archaeology (Liebmann and Rizvi 2010).

However, the dimensions and consequences of postcolonial studies in peripheral regions such as the Canary Islands must be analyzed in greater detail. In the Canary Islands—as a possible consequence of the dynamic processes that have taken place under the burden of Spanish and European colonialism—parallel alternative forms of action–reaction to ways of representing the ethnic, the national, and the historical have not been developed. Consequently, there has been an uncritical application of theories prepared and transmitted principally from the centers of theory production, as has been the tradition in the Canary Islands, where elements of the postcolonial theories produced in the center were not shared with the "eccentric" theories produced in the Canarian archipelago, at least until recent years.[7]

Therefore, not all of today's archaeology falls within the parameters of the postcolonial condition, as has been argued by Gosden (2001) and Hodder (2001). On the contrary, many peripheral archaeologies, as is the case with Canarian archaeology, have been framed by dissimilar sociopolitical environments as the product of their own historical particularities.[8]

The knowledge about the Guanche past that rules today in the Canarian archipelago started to become legitimized with the construction of an official past (mainly since the nationalist prehistory defined during Franco's regime). It has always been the Canarian oligarchy that has invested the greatest efforts in maintaining these conditions, with changing facades and new masks. In this context, history, anthropology, and archaeology have been effective instruments in molding regional consciousness. Obviously, the oligarchy not only governed, and still governs, in the Canary Islands, but also writes its history and dictates the rules that must apply in all social contexts. In this sense, it is clear that the oligarchy, as the colonizer, needed, and still needs, others in order to maintain its status and reproduce itself. This also helps explain why the colonial discourse is still alive in archaeology in the Canary Islands, where postcolonial studies are underrepresented.

Within this context, the recovery of the Canarian Amazigh past is a complex task, as the current colonial discourse developed in the Canarian archipelago can hardly

---

[7] See Farrujia (2010 and 2012) for a detailed discussion of "eccentric" Canarian archaeology in relation to the vanguard centers of capitalist development. See also Díaz-Andreu (2012) for the case of Spanish archaeology in relation to a vanguard center such as Great Britain.

[8] See, for example, the work of Pagán-Jiménez (2004) with regard to the Latin American case, which has many affinities with the Canarian one.

coexist with the evolution of the Maghreb after the so-called "Arab spring,"[9] and the Berber/Amazigh culture movement. This, as defined by Maddy-Weitzman (2011), is an amorphous, multifaceted phenomenon with a clear core demand, namely the affirmation by the state authorities, first and foremost in North Africa, but also in the Amazigh diaspora in Western Europe and North America, of the existence of the Amazigh people as a collective and of the Amazighty of the land of Tamazgha, defined as the area stretching from the Siwa Oasis in the Western Desert of Egypt to the Canary Islands, and as far south as the Sahel. In practical terms, the core demand is for the recognition of Tamazight as an official language in the North African states, and for educational, social, and economic policies to redress the multitude of injustices said to have been inflicted on the Amazigh during the colonial and independence eras.

In Algeria, these efforts are overtly political, owing to the ongoing and long-running confrontation between Kabylia, the territorial and cultural core of resurgent Berberism, and the regime. In Morocco, state–community relations have been less confrontational and less overtly political, but have significantly evolved in this direction in recent years. In France and other European countries (including the Canary Islands), the Amazigh culture movement provides crucial intellectual, moral, and probably financial support for the struggles across the Mediterranean. Fundamentally, the Amazigh culture movement wants nothing less than to reshape the identity of the North African states and fundamentally change the basis of their collective lives (Chafik 2005; El Aissati 2005; Maddy-Weitzman 2006).

Historically, Spain as a sociocultural reality was also constructed by the Amazigh. Muslim Spain was Amazigh from the year 711, as were the Canary Islands, from the middle of the first millennium BC. In addition, many Spanish words are Amazigh, as are many of the Moroccans legally working in Spain today and, naturally, many of the Spanish living in Melilla, the autonomous Spanish city in North Africa. This, in turn, recalls another situation, which is no less important for the fact that it involves a minority issue: Tarifit del Rif, one of the most widely spoken Amazigh languages, is one of the official languages in Melilla, with the same status as the Catalan, Galician, and Basque languages (Maddy-Weitzman 2012). This background implies that the recovery of the Amazigh heritage in the Canary Islands is a politically complex question for the public administration and the pro-Spanish, nationalist political powers. Furthermore, the recovery of this heritage has sociopolitical and cultural implications that transcend the strictly regional environment of the Canarian archipelago, where postcolonial discourse has scarcely affected archaeology.

---

[9] The Arab Spring is a revolutionary wave of demonstrations, protests, and wars occurring in the Arab world that began on December 18th, 2010. To date, rulers have been forced from power in Tunisia, Egypt, Libya, and Yemen, civil uprisings have erupted in Bahrain and Syria, major protests have broken out in Algeria, Iraq, Jordan, Kuwait, Morocco, and Sudan, and minor protests have occurred in Lebanon, Mauritania, Oman, Saudi Arabia, Djibouti, and Western Sahara. There were border clashes in Israel in May 2011, and protests in Iranian Khuzestan by the Arab minority in 2011 as well. Weapons and Tuareg fighters returning from the Libyan civil war fueled the simmering conflict in Mali, which has been described as "fallout" from the Arab Spring in North Africa. The sectarian clashes in Lebanon were described as spillover violence from the Syrian uprising and hence the regional Arab Spring (Maddy-Weitzman, 2011).

4.3   The Internationalization of Archaeological Heritage Management and Indigenous Archaeologies

Despite the fact that postcolonialism has hardly had any impact on Canarian archaeology, the internationalization of archaeological heritage management is common to the Canary Islands and other indigenous archaeologies. The World Heritage Convention of 1972 was a landmark in the internationalization process, establishing the exceptional value of cultural and natural heritage in line with a given set of criteria. As a consequence of the convention, not only did heritage notions and a concept of the past expand worldwide due to the development of the concept of international responsibility for the preservation of the universal heritage, but also a whole "package" of thoughts, doctrines, and categories. Europe (Great Britain, Germany, France, and, to a certain extent, Russia) and the United States, as key players in the world system, became centers for archaeological ideas and practice and their long-term interests and practices contributed towards identifying the most effective methods for investigating the past elsewhere. Therefore, as Lozny (2011) and Willems (2012) have pointed out, the use of German, French, Russian, and, currently, English has made regional ideas global and the global available regionally. Locally significant questions have been answered using ideas and methods available within the global pool of research and globally significant questions have been answered using the local pool of research (data).

The state parties connived to accept the consensus on this "package" through the ratification of international conventions and the nomination of objects and sites reflecting the dominant values. As these notions, categories, and practices had been previously defined, mainly within the historical context of European countries, the archaeology of the Canary Islands is therefore part of this domination over any genuine appropriation of heritage notions and practices. The "dominant language" of international reflection was translated (or, even better, transposed) into new configurations that negotiate with local values. In a certain sense, we may refer to the development of a "single thought" within the framework of archaeological heritage management, using the concept coined by Ramonet (2010).[10] The effects of this approach create a closed, one-dimensional cultural environment favoring a single idea and the imposition of a model (Marcuse 2002).

Within this context, and according to González-Ruibal (2010), postcolonial discourses may amount to little more than another way of using the Other to define Western identities. Politics are reduced to identity issues, a fact that is mirrored in

---

[10] The concept of the "single thought" refers to the translation, in ideological terms, of the claim for universality of the interests of a group of economic forces, in particular international capital, which ultimately monopolize all academic and intellectual forums. The first person to define this "single thought" as a conceptual unit was the German philosopher Arthur Schopenhauer, in his work: *Die Welt als Wille und Vorstellung* (*The World as Will and Representation*), in 1819. Ramonet, who reintroduced the concept in 1995, predicted the dire consequences that would result from widespread adoption of this ideology and listed a series of phenomena that would, in his opinion, contract the notion that a period of prosperity would ensue following the generalization of beliefs, which he described as "single thought". His view has proved prescient.

the social sciences. Postprocessual archaeology echoes these neoliberal concerns particularly well. Whereas Americans, in the processual tradition, are still concerned with political economy, power structures, and statehood, Europeans, following postprocessual trends, usually focus on culture and identity.

However, in the case of indigenous archaeologies, it is important to emphasize that, having grappled with cultural imperialism since the 1960s when heritage tended to promote reductionist views of indigenous cultures, fundamental changes in practice had been introduced in many countries by the 1980s, when indigenous rights discourses led to greater acknowledgment of indigenous ownership and control over their heritage in many postcolonial nations (Ferguson 1996). Nevertheless, indigenous perspectives on archaeology differ throughout the world (North America, Mesoamerica, Scandinavia, Africa, Australia, and New Zealand), as Watkins has analyzed (2005). In this sense, and as a consequence of ethnocide and the gradual disappearance of the Amazigh cultural legacy, it is not possible to compare the case of the Canary Islands with the Australian (Aboriginal), New Zealand (Maori), North American (American Indian, Native American, Alaska Native Corporations, or Native Hawaiian), Canadian (First Nations or Meti), Mesoamerican (Aztec), South American (Inca, Mapuche), or Scandinavian (Sami) contexts. In these international contexts, as Watkins (2005) and Atalay (2006) have shown, the indigenous people have recently become involved in discussing archaeological material from their perspective. In the specific cases of Australia and New Zealand, the Aboriginal peoples are even more involved in using archaeology as a means of re-establishing land tenure. Both approaches are simply not possible in the Canary Islands.[11]

As a result, debates over who owns the past, human remains, and material culture and who has the power to speak for, and write, the stories of the past have all played a prominent role in archaeology. In this long and fierce battle for control over indigenous ancestral and cultural remains and heritage, there have been a number of changes as part of the early steps taken internally towards decolonizing the discipline. These changes included working with native peoples to develop re-burial and repatriation legislation, examples of which include the Native American Graves Protection and Repatriation Act (NAGPRA) and the National Museum of the American Indian (NMAI legislation) analyzed by Ferguson (1996), establishing scholarship funds and training opportunities to increase the number of indigenous people working in archaeology, developing consultation and collaboration between archaeologists and descendant communities and stakeholders, further development of ethical guidelines, and the emergence of research into intellectual and cultural property (Atalay 2006; Ireland 2010).

---

[11] One of the last written testimonies that provides evidence of direct (ethnographic) access to indigenous Canarian traditions dates from the seventeenth century, when the British doctor and merchant Evan Pieugh, who was based in Tenerife, was able to visit certain indigenous burial caves and learn about some indigenous customs, including mummification. The indigenous people of the Güímar valley (in Tenerife) revealed this information to the British doctor as a way of thanking him for treating some members of their community free of charge. As Thomas Sprats noted, in response to the news, "It was a favour rarely, if ever, granted to anyone" (in Farrujia, 2004, p. 103).

Cultural heritage has therefore been a source of conflict between different social groups and the heritage management system is the arena in which postcolonial nations arbitrate contested identity politics. However, this has not been the case in the Canary Islands, where archaeological heritage management has been involved in perpetuating certain aspects of the historical master narratives of Europe. This is why the use of heritage to contest received and collective memory—a particularly common practice in postcolonial nations—simply does not exist in the Canary Islands (at least from an indigenous point of view) due to ethnocide.

In other indigenous contexts worldwide, the historical context and level of indigenous social consciousness that gave rise to indigenous archaeology, as well as the opportunity to draw on the knowledge and experience of indigenous people with a long and painful experience of struggles against colonization, make this an excellent approach to envisaging a decolonized archaeology.

On the basis of these arguments, notions of heritage in nonindigenous contexts, such as the Canary Islands, are deeply intermeshed with European countries and the extent to which they dominate the current treatment of the topic. For example, according to Esposito and Gaulis (2010), in some European languages such as Spanish, Italian, and French, the term used to define heritage (*patrimonio; patrimoine*) has a direct connection with the notion of patrimonial succession and inheritance, as previously noted. The expansion of the premodern idea of the person and of individual property has been used to support the formation of nation states, which based their identity on the idea of a common culture. As Ireland (2010) has pointed out, twentieth and twenty-first century heritage sites are described as cultural anchors, touchstones, symbols of ownership, territory, belonging, and identity. Rather than being understood as linking contemporary societies to death, humility, and frailty, these sites conjure up a vision of cultural immortality. But do indigenous societies share a common culture with postcolonial societies? Obviously not. In this sense, as Ross (1996) has argued, members of indigenous communities have also emphasized the difference between the western concept of heritage as a specific place in a broader natural landscape, and the indigenous concept of heritage, which emphasizes that humankind is not separate from the landscape but is part of an indivisible whole, in which heritage is an everyday lived experience. For the Australian Aboriginals, for example, the history and spirituality of a place is more important than the art itself. If the art is destroyed by natural processes, this does not destroy the importance of the place for them (Veracini, 2006). In the context of the Canary Islands, this same perception is evident in the indigenous Amazigh environment (and also among the North African Imazighen), in particular in the case of the Tindaya Mountain site, discussed later.

It is also important to emphasize that international discourse on heritage is not static. On the basis of the documents produced by UNESCO, this discourse started to change at the end of the 1980s. Proof of this ongoing transformation came in the form of the introduction of "cultural landscapes" as a heritage criterion in 1992, and the Conference of Nara (1994), which questioned the notion of authenticity. Following this, the Convention for the Safeguarding of the Intangible Cultural Heritage (2003) and the Convention on the Protection and Promotion of the Diversity of Cultural Expressions (2005) showed that dominant notions are being reconsidered in relation to non-European contexts. Japan is leading this transformation and the Asian countries appear to be the areas in which criticism of the dominant categories is being voiced, as Esposito and Gaulis have analyzed (2010).

4.4   The Globalization of Archaeology and the Recovery of the Elitist Heritage

In the era of globalization, Western ideology has controlled the archaeological heritage management agenda by analyzing and interpreting indigenous heritage to fit a Western view of culture. In other words, given that cultural identity is inseparable from cultural heritage, the likening of archaeological heritage management to imperialism is justified. Indigenous concerns regarding heritage management are therefore unlikely ever to be fully addressed while heritage managers remain tied to an entirely archaeological and site-based approach to cultural heritage management.

Within this context, as analysis has shown (Willems 2012; Farrujia 2012), a world study carried out by ICOMOS from 1987 to 1993 revealed that Europe, historic cities and religious monuments, Christianity, historical periods, and "elitist" (as opposed to indigenous) architecture were all overrepresented in the World Heritage List and that many archaeological cultures and living cultures, in particular the so-called "traditional cultures," were insufficiently represented. Later, at its 28th meeting in 2004, the World Heritage Committee examined more recent studies of the World Heritage List and the lists prepared by ICOMOS. Both analyses took regional, chronological, geographical, and thematic levels into account with the aim of evaluating the progress of the World Strategy. The ICOMOS study revealed that the absence of particular heritage "realities" from the World Heritage List was due to structural factors (related to World Heritage status and the management and protection of cultural assets) and qualitative factors (related to the way in which the properties were identified, valued and assessed).

In 2005, ICOMOS published a report titled *The World Heritage List: Filling the Gaps—An Action Plan for the Future,* in which the Canary Islands are not addressed. This review of cultural sites in the World Heritage List was undertaken by ICOMOS at the request of the World Heritage Committee in 2000, with the aim of analyzing the cultural sites inscribed in the World Heritage List and Tentative Lists using regional, chronological, geographical, and thematic frameworks. The objective was to provide the State Parties with a clear overview of the current representation of sites according to these categories, and the likely short- to medium-term trends, in order to identify categories that were underrepresented in the List. The study and its findings have a number of implications for the study of Canary Island archaeological landscapes nowadays. The main one is the recognition by the study of the fact that cultural regions do not necessarily correspond to political boundaries, as is the case with the Canarian archipelago, which is located on the margins of Europe, belongs to Spain and therefore to the European Union, but in geographical and archaeological terms is part of Africa. It is therefore not possible to aim for a "balance" in the World Heritage List at State Party or national level. Nevertheless, the broad cultural regions used by UNESCO (Africa, the Arab States, Asia Pacific, Europe/North America, and Latin America/the Caribbean) were used as units of analysis in the typological analysis. Unfortunately, this limits the usefulness of the findings with regard to sites in the Canary Islands. The Canarian archaeological heritage would never fit within the cultural region of "Europe" if this were used as a unit of analysis.

From a chronological–regional point of view, the above-mentioned report on the World Heritage List produced by ICOMOS (2005) attempts to identify significant cultures and civilizations that have emerged and developed in different parts of the globe. In Asia, Africa, Europe, and the Americas the chronological framework developed in the study recognizes that throughout history various "cultures," "empires," or "civilizations" have existed. Obviously, an equivalent chronological framework does not exist within the context of Canarian archaeology, where the "indigenous phase" covers a very brief period, from the middle of the first millennium BC to the rediscovery of the islands by European navigators in the fourteenth century. The 2005 report therefore fails to recognize that there has been a substantial change over time in indigenous cultures like the ones of the Canary Islands and in their social formations and use of the landscape and its resources.

Thus, in the case of the Canary Islands, the heritage recovery process reveals the same inadequacies observed on an international level, even given the fact that there is no indigenous archaeology in the Canary Islands, but instead a strong colonial influence on historical and archaeological discourses. In this sense, the history that has been preserved in the Canarian archipelago tends to be the history of the ruling classes, from the conquest of the islands onwards. The monuments that have been preserved are those associated with the cultural events and production of the ruling classes (palaces, churches, stately homes, mansions, etc.). The language of power is "urbanized" and made into heritage. The history of the dominated classes, in this case the Canarian indigenous people, is rarely preserved. Secondly, as in the international context, the Western, European-style historical heritage is effectively richer, more elaborate, and more "monumental." In undervaluing the heritage legacy that predates the conquest of the Canarian archipelago, countless cultural creations that were not assimilated by the elites have been lost, and historical events that are significant and important in understanding the history and identity of the Canarian archipelago itself have been forgotten.

Given the situation in the Canary Islands, where the "elitist" heritage is the main priority, it may be said that this scenario reveals clear affinities with the international context as described by Disko (2010), inasmuch as out of the 890 properties designated World Heritage sites under the UNESCO 1972 World Heritage Convention, as of February 2010 only a few are located in indigenous territories or areas in which indigenous peoples have rights of ownership, access, or use. Although it would be difficult to establish the exact number of these indigenous sites in the World Heritage List and this would require careful analysis, it is estimated that there are between 70 and 100 such sites (Disko 2010). The vast majority of them are inscribed as "natural sites," with no reference to the indigenous culture or the existence of indigenous peoples in the justification for their inclusion.

In the Canary Islands, heritage is seen not only as a global discourse but also a discourse of globalization, through its promotion of the idea of heritage as material and authentic, as argued by Ireland (2002, 2010) in a wider context. Heritage thus occupies a dual position, as both a cause and effect of cultural globalization. Yet heritage, in a general sense, is linked to territory and memory, which are both aspects of identity. In the case of the Canary Islands and its indigenous past, and to paraphrase François Hartog (2004, p. 6), it is not a matter of an obvious and affirmative identity but an inconvenient identity that runs the risk of disappearing or has, to a great extent, been forgotten, erased, or repressed: an identity in search of itself, which has to be exhumed, reassembled, or even invented. However, this recovery of the Canarian indigenous or insular Amazigh past should not be directed towards the search for new commercial products, because in other contexts such as Mexico (see Nalda 2004) this has condemned research and the entire focus of the archaeology to the recovery of objects of aesthetic value and to valuing the most monumental sites and those of outstanding aesthetic value.

According to Forbes, Page, and Perez (2009) and Lozny (2011, Introduction), this scenario clearly reflects that the fact that current research trends and the preservation of cultural heritage worldwide indicate a globalized approach to the past and archaeology as the only discipline for studying past societies not recorded through script. In this context, archaeology becomes nationless and cultural heritage is understood as global, rather than local, heritage. It is assumed that any interest in the past represented at nation state level will be replaced by a more global approach. Therefore, the recent approach to cultural heritage research and preservation has contributed towards the globalization of archaeology, in an attempt to unify goals and direct actions to preserve what now counts as world heritage rather than just national heritage. The key problem is how this globalized approach should be forged, the theory and practice that should be followed, and, more generally, what we want to know about the past and how we are going to answer these questions.

As Willems (2012) has pointed out, it seems that we are currently in a phase in which the predominant European heritage regime is being supplemented, if not gradually superseded, by a new transnational heritage regime. This is a regime that combines ethical frameworks from global organizations, both private corporations and public bodies, and does not rely solely on experts as stewards or caretakers but actively seeks to empower local populations. However, the international community of heritage experts is only just becoming aware of this trend and therefore most of the consequences still need to be examined.

The following sections focus on the regional context in order to analyze examples of heritage management in the Canary Islands in which the indigenous heritage has been ignored or marginalized, as well as other cases in which it has been successfully recovered. The negative examples are represented by San Cristóbal de La Laguna and Aguere (Tenerife) and the Tindaya Mountain (Fuerteventura). Both cases show how the heritage policy in the Canary Islands has focused on recovering the historic or "elitist" heritage. By failing to include the precolonial heritage, which also defines the historical evolution of the Canarian archipelago, in the discourse this has made it impossible to place any value on cultural diversity.

The positive examples in which the indigenous legacy is valued are represented by the cases of the Cueva Pintada de Gáldar (Gran Canaria), El Júlan (El Hierro), and La Zarza y La Zarcita and Belmaco (La Palma), all sites that have been recovered and preserved to ensure they are valued and accessible to the public. However, it is important to note that all the sites offer a partial reading of the indigenous Canarian past, because they are based on a particular type of (rock) site and do not include any other defining features of the indigenous societies (such as habitat, burial customs, or economic practices). In other words, they have helped to create an "aesthetic" of the indigenous past on the basis of rock art motifs. The case of the Cueva Pintada de Gáldar, as becomes clear later, offers a more inclusive vision of the indigenous past, although the rock art remains the centerpiece of its offer.

4.5   Excluding the Indigenous Archaeological Heritage: The Case of Aguere (Tenerife)

The Castilian settlers founded the first capital of Tenerife, San Cristóbal de La Laguna (Aguere), in 1496.[12] There were several reasons for basing the city on this part of the island. It was situated far away from the coast and so could avoid attacks from pirates, it was a stopping-off point for those traveling from one side of the island to the other, it had a good climate and fertile soil for crops and grazing, and drinking water was available in the vicinity.

According to some authors such as Rodríguez Yanez (1997), the first urban development in La Laguna was different from the recognized forms of Renaissance planning in that it simply responded to immediate needs, but still embodied the model of the city in fashion at the time, which was defined by a carefully planned regularity. However, according to Navarro Segura (1999), La Laguna was designed as the archetype for the city-territory. It was the first example of a nonfortified city designed and built according to a plan influenced by navigational aids and science, and organized in accordance with a new peaceful social order inspired by the millenary religious doctrine of the year 1500 (please see Fig. 4.1). The plan of the city can be read as a compass rose, in which the cardinal points correspond to specific places in the city and certain points are also related to the whole. It had a symbolic meaning and can be interpreted as a period navigational chart or map of the constellations.

Due to its urban development designs and historical and heritage values, on December 2nd, 1999 the UNESCO World Heritage Committee meeting in Marrakech (Morocco) declared the city of San Cristóbal de La Laguna a World Heritage Site. The criteria used to justify this distinction were essentially:

---

[12] Aguere is an indigenous toponym that means "lake" and refers to the natural lake in the municipality which dried up in the second half of the nineteenth century. The actual name of the city, La Laguna, comes from this indigenous legacy. The city is also known as "Ciudad de Los Adelantados," as Adelantado (Captain General) Alonso Fernández de Lugo (the founder of La Laguna) and his descendants had their residence there.

Fig. 4.1 Examples of the "elitist" architecture of San Cristóbal de La Laguna (Tenerife), declared a World Heritage Site on December 2nd, 1999

a. The concept of La Laguna as a historical complex that was the archetype for the "city-territory", the first example of a nonfortified colonial city and the immediate predecessor to the new foundations in the Americas.
b. The fact that city was designed on the basis of a complete plan based on philosophical principles and executed using the navigational and scientific knowledge of the time.
c. The fact that its original layout, dating from the year 1500, has remained intact.
d. Around 600 buildings that are examples of Mudejar architecture have been preserved in good condition.
e. It serves as a living example of the interchanges between European culture and American culture, with which it has maintained constant links.

The archaeological heritage of the indigenous people of Aguere of Amazigh origin, which existed on the island prior to its conquest and colonization by the kingdom of Castile was not one of the criteria taken into consideration when the Ciudad de los Adelantados was declared a World Heritage Site. In other words, the indigenous legacy was not included in the heritage assets that define the identity of the municipality.

It may be considered that this omission is due to the adoption by the administration of a heritage policy that invests in the recovery of an elitist heritage and, on the other hand, to the lack of any heritage policy that values archaeological sites in the municipality. The entire construction of the historic city offers an archaeological dimension—the possibility of its being documented using archaeological methods—which in many cases, including this example, is not being sufficiently explored, as is analyzed in the next section.

4.5.1   Aguere and Archaeology

From a spatial and geographical point of view, certain ethnohistorical sources (and the information contained in particular division dates) indicate that at the time of the conquest of Tenerife in 1496, the island was divided into nine *menceyatos* or native kingdoms. Each *menceyato* represented an area of land within a well-defined natural district that had sufficient resources to meet the needs of the human group that lived there. In the case of Tenerife the *menceyatos* were Anaga, Tegueste, Tacorón, Taoro, Icod, Daute, Adeje, Abona, and Güímar.

As Luis Diego Cuscoy notes in his classic work *Los guanches*: *Vida y cultura del primitivo habitante de Tenerife* (1968), the *menceyato* of Tegueste included Punta del Hidalgo, Las Canteras, la Vega de La Laguna, El Púlpito, El Portezuelo, and Punta del Viento and, in the western sector, the whole of Valle de Guerra and Valle del Boquerón, meaning that the municipality of La Laguna formed part of the Tegueste *menceyato*. Modern locations such as Punta del Hidalgo, Bajamar, Tejina, el Caserio de Milán, Tegueste itself, and Pedro Álvarez fall within the boundaries of this *menceyato* and it is therefore clear that these places and houses have been built on areas formerly inhabited by the Guanche and, in some cases (Tejina or the town of Tegueste), primitive cave settlements, the main type of dwelling used by the Guanche.

However, in the case of la Vega de La Laguna, according to Diego Cuscoy the area was not designated a living area in indigenous times but instead served as pasture land. Therefore, in the historic center of La Laguna and the outskirts of La Vega no residential archaeological sites have been documented. In addition to the fact that it was used as grazing land, this can also be explained by the following:

a. The fact that permanent inhabited areas are very close (e.g., Barranco de Agua de Dios, in Tegueste).
b. The existence of a significant wooded area descending from the Las Mercedes mountains almost to the center of La Laguna, which made the area virtually uninhabitable.
c. The geography of the area, because the land is flat and contains no caves that could have been used as dwellings.
d. The existence of La Laguna lake, which reduced the habitable area and made La Laguna a (spring) water supply point. The pasture land in La Vega de La Laguna was used, both in indigenous and postconquest times, by shepherds from Tegueste.

The historic center of La Laguna was not therefore "raised" on an indigenous settlement. However, it should be noted that very few archaeological interventions have been carried out in the municipality and the area surrounding the historic center, and it may be said that La Laguna is one of the least well-studied areas of the island from an archaeological point of view, together with other municipalities such as Arafo and El Rosario. Preventive archaeology has not been developed in the municipality of La Laguna, meaning that it is impossible to assess the extent of the potential irreversible loss of historic or prehistoric remains in the subsoil that may have been affected by urban planning projects, new building work, renovation work, and the like.[13]

Given this situation, the small amount of archaeological fieldwork carried out in the municipality has led to other indigenous sites being documented in the vicinity of the historic center, such as the rock art sites. These sites consist of graphic representations engraved into the rocks by the indigenous people in the form of motifs that are abstract (drawn without a clear geometry), geometric (crosses, circles, checkered squares, suns, etc.), and figurative or representational (human figures, footprints [podomorphs], animals [horses, etc.]) as well as representations of objects (boats, etc.). The significance of these sites is still being studied today, because the motifs engraved into the stone had a very profound cultural meaning for the societies that created them. The "message" these engraved motifs conveyed has still not been satisfactorily explained, hence for some authors certain sites refer to a type of territorial border, in addition to the religious significance that particular rock sites would also appear to have (Tejera et al. 2008).

This type of site, which exists in significant numbers in the municipality of La Laguna, remained undiscovered until the early 1980s, although the numbers have risen since then, particularly towards the end of this decade. By the time the *Inventario del Patrimonio Arqueológico de las Canarias Occidentales* was published by Juan Francisco Navarro Mederos in 1989, various rock art sites in La Laguna had been catalogued, and their numbers increased in the years that followed. With regard to these sites, it is important to highlight the following aspects, which are also valid for other indigenous sites of a different nature and typology (natural and burial caves, shelters, and huts, etc.) documented in La Laguna:

a. Their worrying state of conservation, due to the evident damage in some cases and the threat of disappearance in others.
b. Clear indications of North African Imazighen influences on the archaeological heritage, therefore representing evidence of a considerable interchange of human values during a particular period of time and in a specific cultural area (the Canary Islands).
c. Their testimony to the indigenous culture prior to the conquest and colonization of Tenerife in 1496, offering exceptional evidence of a lost cultural tradition.
d. Their location, in general, in areas of great landscape value.

---

[13] The historic center of La Laguna lacks a specific inventory of the archaeological assets in the urban zone. The lack of knowledge and hierarchical structure of the urban archaeological heritage prevents any interrelation between the archaeological maps and urban planning designed to protect the urban historic landscape (Mestre, 2012). It is therefore not surprising that the Special Protection Plan for the La Laguna Historical Complex (July, 2005) contains no references to the archaeological heritage. The Plan is available at: http://www. gerenciaurbanismo.com/gerencia/GERENCIA/published/DEFAULT/planeamiento/pecasco_ad/1_ memord/memord_1.pdf

e. The fact that they therefore meet many of the criteria for inclusion in the World Heritage List, as established in the "Convention Concerning the Protection of the World Cultural and Natural Heritage", approved by UNESCO in November 1972. However, it is not enough for an area to offer outstanding value to humanity in order to achieve preservation status; political will is also required, as it has been pointed out by Mulvaney and Hicks (2012) in analyzing the case of the Dampier Archipelago (Australia), which presents clear affinities with the problematic described for La Laguna.

Outside the historic center of the municipality of La Laguna, the archaeological situation offers even greater riches and typological variety, inasmuch as the areas that were most densely populated in indigenous times are found in Barranco de Milán, from Tejina to the sea, the Punta del Hidalgo-Bajamar coastline, and the Valle de Guerra coast. According to the *Inventario del Patrimonio Arqueológico de las Canarias Occidentales* (1989), the municipality of La Laguna has six archaeological zones distributed between the coast and the interior that are of great heritage value. Within these zones, cave dwellings and dry stone huts, temporary/seasonal herdsmen sites, mounds of shells, and small burial caves have been recorded. The following archaeological zones merit special attention: Barranco de Milán, due to the important concentration of cave dwellings and therefore the existence of a settlement cluster; Lomo de La Fuente-Lomo de Lugo, due to the presence of specific rock art sites, especially those with groove and cup motifs associated either with shelters or huts; Montaña de Guerra, which contains large cave dwellings and huts, reflecting a well-established settlement. The latter zone also contains the Becerril (Barranco de Santos) mass burial cave studied by Juan Álvarez Delgado (1944–1945). The remains of 50 individuals have been recorded in this site.

The archaeological heritage of La Laguna is therefore significant enough to be enhanced by opening museums or sites that can be visited, thus ensuring not only their protection and conservation but also their recognition by society. Encouraging knowledge of the archaeological heritage would lead to an interest in its conservation. All of this would obviously have a positive impact on the cultural opportunities the municipality can offer and their decentralization, because the heritage assets are not exclusively limited to the historic center but may extend to areas immediately outside the center (where there are many rock art sites) or those farther away, such as Valle Guerra (Montaña de Guerra, La Barranquera).

4.5.2   Valuing the Indigenous Heritage: Archaeological Parks?

Since the beginning of the 1990s the term "archaeological park" has become common although its use is not unproblematic, basically due to a lack of consensus on what such areas should contain, as Saco del Valle has pointed out (2001). However, in general terms, an archaeological park is a physical space containing the following elements:

a. The presence of one or more assets of recognized cultural interest, in compliance with the current legislation on historic heritage
b. Suitable environmental conditions to enable the public to observe, enjoy, and understand the area

In recent years in Spain there has been a drive towards the creation of new archaeological parks, together with the creation of paleontological parks. They all take the site as a starting point and their development extends beyond merely scientific concerns (Querol 2010). Various autonomous communities rely on their own legislation in this area, in order to:

a. Protect, improve, and transmit to future generations the outstanding features of the archaeological heritage, which relies on suitable environmental conditions for this to be accomplished.
b. Provide more information on heritage, so that it can be better appreciated by citizens.
c. Encourage sustainable development compatible with the conservation and dissemination of the cultural and natural assets in the park.
d. Provide for shared responsibility and cooperation with public bodies.

At present, Tenerife has no archaeological parks.[14] However, in the case of La Laguna there are specific examples of sites whose value could be enhanced if they were developed as archaeological parks. This is the case, for example, with the La Barranquera archaeological zone, a substantial coastal settlement consisting of cave dwellings and dry stone huts, generally in rocky areas, as well as small temporary/seasonal herdsmen sites, mounds of shells, and small burial caves.

Nevertheless, the heritage policy for La Laguna stands apart from the model attempted by the rest of Spain and some of the other Canary Islands, where in the last decade there has been a reassessment of concepts such as cultural landscape and cultural parks and an evaluation of the archaeological heritage within the framework of territorial planning strategies, as is argued in the forthcoming pages. The cultural landscape and cultural park have begun to be used effectively in a series of projects that, within a national and European context, consider the protection of the archaeological heritage should include a serious commitment on the part of those responsible for historical research and those responsible for land planning (the municipal, district, and regional authorities).

4.5.3 Archaeology and the Local Community

Within this context, the archaeologist's responsibility for protecting and developing the archaeological heritage, in collaboration with various specialists and in cooperation with local communities, as analyzed by Marciniak (2000) and Smith and

---

[14] In the case of the island of Tenerife, its Archaeological Museum is the driving force behind almost 100% of the diffusion and dissemination of the archaeological heritage on the island. Although many archaeological zones in Tenerife are protected as BICs, none have user value.

Waterton (2009), should also be emphasized. In the case of La Laguna, the *Historia, Arte e identidad* project developed by the Historical Heritage Councillor on the La Laguna City Council from February to July 2008 revealed a demand on the part of the community for access to information on the indigenous heritage.[15] The project included conferences held in different civic centers that aimed to publicize the architectural, ethnographic, artistic, and archaeological assets within the municipality. Parallel to this, guided group tours were offered to places of historical–artistic interest linked to the themes of the conferences. In the case of the conferences on Guanche or Amazigh archaeology in the municipality, the surveys completed by the public who attended revealed various issues, including the community's lack of knowledge of the Guanche culture in the municipality and the consequent demand for guided tours of its archaeological sites. However, these field trips did not take place, because there were no sites in the municipality that afforded the conditions for such visits. This explains to a great extent why all the respondents were able to list the essentially architectural elements of the municipal heritage as clear "landmarks" but not the archaeological heritage that predated the conquest.

Efforts should therefore be made to involve the local community on a more active basis, ensuring that it shares the results of research work, presented in accessible language, and ensuring its involvement in the management of the archaeological heritage or in research (e.g., by collaborating in some of the excavation work), awareness-raising activities, the development of tourism, and controlling the impact created by major projects, all aspects that have been addressed, in a wider context, by Mauch and Smith (2010) and Jay Stottman (2010). Only in this way can social awareness of the importance of protecting the natural and cultural heritage be developed, and can archaeology reach the public and enable it to become involved with it. It is therefore necessary to remove the educational and material barriers that prevent the vast majority of the population from having access to this type of cultural asset and it is also important to preserve and transmit the cultural production that belongs to the people, guaranteeing them access to tools that can facilitate this and enable it to be communicated and transmitted (Ribeiro Durham 1998).

In the case of the historical heritage in the center of La Laguna, the task of dissemination developed by the municipal administration has encouraged the active involvement of the local community in various kinds of activities, such as open days in historic buildings, guided tours of the historic center, themed routes (the La Laguna convents, La Laguna palaces, etc.), exhibitions and talks, conferences, and congresses. It is important to bear in mind that the city is seen by the local community as its own local residential space (De Certeau 2008). The heritage of the historic center is directly related to the history of the local community and its everyday life and thus there is a feeling of belonging and identification with this type of cultural asset, which is not the case, or at least not on the same scale, with the Guanche heritage in La Laguna.

---

[15] As in the Canary Islands there are no indigenous populations nowadays, the local community is mainly integrated by people of Spanish origins (born in the Canary Islands).

Fig. 4.2 View of the Tindaya Mountain (La Oliva, Fuerteventura). Photograph: Tarek Ode

As a result, an approach that advocates valuing the archaeological heritage in terms of landscape and involving the community has not been established in areas such as La Laguna, where the local authority has invested in focusing on the recovery of the elitist, historical, and predominantly architectural heritage.

Social and residential space is the result of an ongoing conflict between power and resistance to power, a product of the operations that guide it, locate it in time and space, and allow it to function (Foucault 1977). In this sense, the community, citizens, and archaeologists have the potential to open up an original creative space that can contribute towards the recovery and appreciation of the Guanche heritage from this alternative perspective.

4.6   Heritage Speculation: The Case of the Tindaya Mountain (Fuerteventura)

Unlike Tenerife, the island of Fuerteventura has an Interpretation Centre in Poblado de La Atalayita (Antigua), a settlement first occupied in indigenous times then reused by shepherds following the conquest of the island. In addition to the Interpretation Centre, which provides visitors with information on the excavations and the remains that have been recovered, numerous structures can be observed in the surrounding area, such as cave dwellings, underground or semi-excavated houses, and a traditional dwelling. The island also has an Archaeological Museum (Betancuria), based in a traditional building which reopened in 2007 after it had been restored and fully renovated. Its two rooms provide visitors with information on the life, customs, and beliefs of the ancient indigenous populations.

This heritage initiative contrasts radically with the case of the Tindaya Mountain (La Oliva, Fuerteventura; Fig. 4.2) which, in terms of its natural and cultural value, is unique in the Canary Islands and for which it has earned: (a) the classification of Asset of Cultural Interest (BIC), affording it the highest level of protection and recognition that can be granted under Law 16/85 of 25 June on the Spanish Historical Heritage, and (b) classification as a Natural Monument, under Law 12/1994 of 19 December on Natural Sites in the Canary Islands. However, this has not prevented threats to the mountain and its values in the form of plans, ongoing since 1994, to develop an artistic project designed by the well-known Basque sculptor Eduardo Chillida (1924–2002).

4.6.1   The Tindaya Archaeological Assets

The year 1977 marked the starting point in the study of rock art in Fuerteventura, when the most important archaeological site on the island was discovered, namely Tindaya Mountain, a trachyte plug whose summit stands 400 m above sea level. Studies by Hernández Pérez and Martín Socas (1980) had a decisive influence on subsequent discoveries on the island, inasmuch as no previous evidence of rock art had been found in Fuerteventura. In other words, the dissemination of scientific information on Tindaya quickly became a reference point for understanding rock art in Fuerteventura.

The archaeological assets in Tindaya, as Perera Betancort has noted (1996), consist of a series of podomorph rock engravings (in other words, outlines of human feet that appear to be anatomically well executed) together with many other geometrical designs which appear to feature only rectangular motifs but are essentially more schematic representations of podomorphs. There are also motifs that do not form clear geometrical shapes and have been interpreted as irregular, unfinished engravings, fragmented or obliterated by erosion and lichens. All the engravings, which have clear parallels with examples in North Africa (the Western Sahara, the Moroccan Atlas region, and Tassili Nager in Algeria), were created using pecking techniques in some cases and incision in others, and are found in the mid and highest slopes of the mountain. The sacred nature of the mountain can also be established from comparison with similar sites documented in North Africa, for example, in the Atlas region. In the North African Amazigh context, podomorph engravings and the places where they are found have a strong magical significance (Hachid 2000). The engravings of feet serve to make the areas sacred, although it is not the engravings that are sacred, but the space itself.

Tindaya is the largest podomorph rock art site in the Canary Islands, with more than 217 footprints recorded, arranged in 52 panels, to which 7 other bases displaying 21 prints can be added, that have been missing from the site for two years and which the administration has failed to investigate or recover (please see Fig. 4.3.) At present, looting still affects other panels in the site, where sections have been chipped off.

However, the most significant fact about Tindaya, as Perera, Belmonte, Esteban, and Tejera have noted (1996), is that the engravings are not randomly distributed, inasmuch as 80% of them are set at angles ranging from 225 to 270° Within these coordinates lie Pico del Teide, in Tenerife (the highest mountain in Spanish territory,

Fig. 4.3 Examples of panels of podomorph engravings. Tindaya Mountain (La Oliva, Fuerteventura). Photograph: Tarek Ode

standing 3,717 m above sea level) and Pico de las Nieves, in Gran Canaria (1,949 m high), which can be seen from the top of Tindaya on a clear day. Moreover, this range includes the sunset during the winter solstice, the major and minor lunar standstills, the full moon following the summer solstice, the new moon following the winter solstice, and, more generally, the autumn and winter sunsets between the equinoxes when the sun sets exactly in the east (270°) and the winter solstice. The remaining 20% of the engravings are not randomly distributed either, but tend to cluster around other cardinal points. They also feature podomorphs that, unless in pairs, are arranged in panels in which the engravings are all distributed in the dominant direction.

Various unexcavated funerary structures can also be found in Tindaya, together with an archaeological record located in the same middle and upper zones and in various archaeological sites at the base where the following surface finds have been documented: pieces of ceramics, fragments of ceramic idols, countless lithic items, malacological material, and so on. Among these sites at the foot of the mountain, special mention should be made of Majada de los Negrines on the northern side, which contains various dry stone residential structures, two of which are of a considerable size, and are built from stone blocks with an oval ground plan (Perera 1996).

Tindaya was also a site where games, dances, and other undetermined events took place, as reflected in the oral or ethnographic tradition, which may explain the merging of ancient indigenous traditions with the legends of the inhabitants of the islands during the colonial period. The Cueva del Bailadero de Las Brujas can be found in the area surrounding Tindaya where, according to tradition men and women gathered for games, and the Cueva del Bailadero de Los Pastores, where local boys and girls learned to dance (Perera 1996; Tejera et al. 2008, p. 111).

Among all these cultural assets, only the podomorph engravings are expressly protected, because they are recognized as Asset of Cultural Interest under Article 40.2 of the LPHE. In addition to their beauty and geomorphological structure, the natural assets, categorized as a Natural Monument, also contain an endemism, *Caralluma burchardii*, which is protected under regional legislation. Tindaya also has mining interests, derived directly from trachyte, its main natural and geological asset. There are several quarries, currently closed, on the mountainside where this material is extracted for use, mainly to decorate the facades of buildings.

4.6.2   Eduardo Chillida's Art Project in Tindaya

In 1985, the sculptor Eduardo Chillida announced in an interview that he was thinking of creating a monument inside a mountain. Almost a decade later, after searching in various places all over the world and rejecting sites in Finland, Switzerland, and Sicily, Chillida chose the Tindaya Mountain for his project, the *Monumento a la tolerancia*. From the outset it had the backing of the Canarian government, which bought the mining rights for the interior of the mountain from the Cabo Verde S.A. company for five million euros.

Chillida's project aimed to empty the Tindaya Mountain in order to create a vast central chamber in the shape of a cube, with each side measuring 50 m. It would be entered via a passageway 70–80 m high and 15 m wide and two shafts approximately 25 m wide would be set into the upper part of the cube, extending from the top of the chamber to the slopes at the top of the mountain. Defined as the sun and moon shafts, they would provide natural lighting for the central chamber. They would be set in the upper corners opposite the entrance and emerge on the surface of the mountain, one on the north side and one in the south (Giráldez 2007).

Chillida's idea was that Fuerteventura would have a permanent work of art of international standing that would link humanity to the natural elements, such as the sun, the moon, and the sea. The project was inspired by a line of poetry ("Deep is the air") from the *Cántico* by Jorge Guillén, and the sculptor's own vision of a mountain stripped of its interior to enable it to be filled with space in homage to the smallness that unites humanity, as a monument to tolerance and a work of art for the Canarian people.

With the realization of this project, according to the government of the Canary Islands, Fuerteventura would have a cultural attraction that would enhance the island itself and the Canarian archipelago, because it could become a center of attraction to be added to those already existing in Fuerteventura, one of the islands with the greatest present-day tourism potential. On the basis of these arguments, on May 24th, 1996 the Council of the Canarian government declared the project designed by Eduardo Chillida for the Tindaya Mountain an item of "Interest to the Canary Islands," given: (a) its artistic value, as a work produced at the peak of Eduardo Chillida's career, a figure recognized internationally as one of the most important sculptors in the world; (b) its value to tourism, because the existence of a monumental sculpture of this kind in the vicinity of a major international destination such as the Canary Islands would serve as an impetus for a form of tourism that was very important to the archipelago; (c) its social value, because the development required to create the monument in a protected area would bring social and economic benefits to the surrounding areas, encourage the creation of services, and generate employment); (d) its ecological value, because the creation of the sculpture would provide a final solution for the surface mining (quarrying) that had been developed legally and with authorization for years, in detriment to the now-protected natural surroundings (Navarro Segura 2002; Giráldez 2007).

In 1996 the Tindaya Mountain Study Commission, consisting of experts in the fields of archaeology and law, was created at the request of the Fuerteventura Island Council. In the opinion of the commission, the mountain, declared a Natural

Monument and BIC, was not appropriate for Chillida's project. Only one year later, in 1997, the anticorruption authorities investigated alleged irregularities concerning the purchase of the mine. Chillida, meanwhile, announced that he had abandoned the project, due to the protests made by archaeologists, geologists, ecology groups, and the opposition of the Fuerteventura Council. In 1997, however, the government of the Canary Islands launched an international bid for tender for the construction of the monument and in 1998 the project was awarded. Even after Chillida's death in 2002, the government of the Canary Islands stated its firm intention to go ahead with building the monument, with work commencing in February 2009, although in 2008 a report from the ombudsman had questioned the value of the project and raised doubts about the geotechnical study carried out by the construction company. Just two years later, in 2010, the ombudsman called for a halt to the Tindaya project, which has still not been rejected by the Canarian government.

4.6.3 Neglect of the Indigenous Heritage

As in the case of San Cristóbal de La Laguna (Aguere), the case of the Tindaya Mountain clearly shows how Western heritage values, which are essentially European in outlook, govern heritage management in the Canary Islands. Heritage items such as rock engravings, settlements, and indigenous funerary structures have been subordinated to the monumental nature of the Chillida project. "Land planning" criteria have given way to speculation and to placing value on an elitist *ex novo* heritage (represented by the *Monumento a la tolerancia* project) which, in Tindaya, leads to an undervaluing of the indigenous heritage, changes to the natural surroundings, and threats to the integrity of the archaeological sites on the mountain as a result of the sculpture planned for its interior. In this regard, the creation of one of the tunnels or shafts for the sculpture project, as described in the Special Protection Plan (Giráldez 2007), affects the area where the engravings and burial structures lie.

Moreover, the case of Tindaya reveals how the heritage management approach adopted by the Canarian authorities is clearly influenced by tourism, the main economic sector in the Canary Islands. In the case of Fuerteventura, the island has moved from depending exclusively on the primary sector to basing its economy on tourism, essentially since the 1960s, with the consequent overexploitation of the environment (involving hotels, urban developments, roads, and services). Attracting more tourists and increasing the economic benefits are the guiding forces behind a heritage policy that essentially presupposes the deterioration of the indigenous heritage and fails to preserve an area protected by law and considered sacred by the early settlers in Fuerteventura. The individuals responsible for the footprint engravings and burial structure chose Tindaya because of the special significance the mountain had for them.[16]

---

[16] A similar problematic can be found in Canada, where aboriginal burial grounds throughout the country are threatened by developments associated with construction projects, road-building, dredging, and flooding. Many of the provincial laws protecting cemeteries mention aboriginal burial sites, however, in practice these laws have done little to prevent the desecration of aboriginal burial grounds (Blair, 2005).

Tourism developments should not therefore be reduced to a matter of economic benefits and more infrastructure: the ethics associated with appreciating the value of these sites should be given priority. If tourism is not carefully and effectively managed in areas that contain archaeological materials, the scientific and historical values that can only be appreciated through a careful study of such materials will be lost irretrievably, together with the material itself. This is not speculation; there is ample evidence that the archaeological record has been increasingly compromised in recent decades as the numbers of visitors to archaeological/cultural sites have grown (Pinter 2005; Binoy 2011).

It is therefore reasonable that the mountain should be preserved as it was known to the indigenous people of Fuerteventura. If Chillida's sculpture project is finally authorized (the mining activity has been halted), it would alter the natural features of the mountain and irreversibly change the most important and significant feature in the entire area. From a legal point of view, in order to ensure proper conservation of cultural assets the LPHE establishes a set of absolute bans or nonauthorizable measures that include the displacement or removal of all immovable Assets of Cultural Interest. The preservation of the Tindaya Mountain and its natural and cultural assets represents an instrument for the promotion of culture through recognition of the indigenous heritage and therefore constitutes a cultural offer based on the study of the precolonial past of the island.

The social, ecological, and professional movement to save Tindaya is a clear example of collective resistance on the part of the local community in the face of heritage directives issued by the government of the Canary Islands, which seems to be turning its back on the cultural and natural assets of the sacred Tindaya Mountain. This resistance movement has made it clear that the actions of the public administration should comply with the aforementioned legal principles. It also shows that the Chillida project is not compatible with the preservation of the Tindaya Mountain, a symbol of the identity of a community and a landmark in its history. It clearly reflects how the value of archaeological heritage assets is proportional to the importance that the community ascribes to them, rather than how they are categorized by the public administration.

4.7   Positive Management of the Indigenous Heritage in the Canary Islands

The cases of Aguere and Tindaya reveal the nature of the archaeology management model that has been adopted for the Canary Islands by the public administration. However, there are other examples within the Canarian context in which the management of the indigenous heritage has been satisfactory. The greater political sensitivity towards indigenous remains in islands such as Gran Canaria, El Hierro, and La Palma has made it possible for specific sites in which the central feature is rock art to be appreciated.

Fig. 4.4 View of the Cueva Pintada de Gáldar (decorated chamber), Gran Canaria. Photograph: Javier Betancor. ©Cabildo de Gran Canaria

4.7.1 La Cueva Pintada de Gáldar (Gran Canaria)

The Cueva Pintada de Gáldar (Fig. 4.4) is a rock chamber decorated with geometric paintings that lends its name to the present-day archaeological zone and museum center associated with the cave. According to Onrubia, Rodríguez, Saenz, and Antona (2007, p. 189), the Gáldar painted motifs are "the most authentic manifestation of pre-Hispanic murals, an exceptional testimony to the artistic and symbolic expression of the early Canarians."

The site is located in Gáldar, the *Agaldar* of indigenous times, which was the most important center of political power in Gran Canaria, according to what can be deduced from the ethnohistorical sources produced by Europeans between the fourteenth and fifteenth centuries. Gáldar was the seat of the major island assemblies and the residence of the *guanartemes*, the largest and most influential family in the precolonial era (Onrubia 2003).

The Cueva Pintada de Gáldar was discovered in 1862 and various contemporary witness accounts emphasize that it contained mummies, ceramics, and other archaeological items. From the time when it was discovered, the site featured significantly in archaeological literature on the Canary Islands from the end of the nineteenth century up to the present day (Onrubia et al. 2007; Farrujia 2009). It also played a central role in the various hypotheses developed during the same period of time to explain the indigenous settlements on the Canary Islands, particularly in the case of the theories developed in support of the Mediterranean roots of the indigenous populations (Farrujia 2004).

On April 29th, 1972 the site was opened to the public and on May 5th of the same year, on the basis of Decree 1434/1972, it was declared a Historical–Artistic National Monument (and is now an archaeological zone BIC). However, problems in preserving the polychrome chamber led to the site being closed to the public until the summer of 1982, only a decade after it was officially opened as an archaeological site. It reopened on July 26th, 2006, heralding a new phase in which, among other challenges, the center is facing the problem of establishing itself as a social space in which research, conservation, and dissemination remain the keystones of a coherent program of heritage work.

Fig. 4.5 An indigenous house in the Cueva Pintada de Gáldar Archaeological Park and Museum (Gran Canaria). Photograph: Javier Betancor. ©Cabildo de Gran Canaria

Fig. 4.6 Detail of the first vertical communications node (stairs and lift, essential for access). The site, enclosure, covering, and walkways can also be seen. Photograph: Javier Betancor. ©Cabildo de Gran Canaria

- The Cueva Pintada de Gáldar Archaeological Assets

The various excavations undertaken since 1987 have revealed an important indigenous settlement based in the cave complex of the same name and consisting of approximately 50 semi-underground stone houses and cave dwellings (please see Figs. 4.5 and 4.6). The chronology for the settlement, for which at least two very different phases of occupation have been documented, ranges from the twelfth to the fifteenth century. In material terms, in addition to the indigenous items (ceramics, idols, millstones, bone, and lithic industry), imported materials have also been documented, mainly originating from mainland Spain as a result of contacts between the indigenous population and the colonialists. Ceramics produced using a wheel and decorated with glass and varnish, and metal items (coins, swords, knives, horseshoes, thimbles, nails, etc.) form part of the range of imported materials (Onrubia et al. 2007).

In the specific case of the rock chamber, it is important to note that decorating the walls of dwellings, burial caves, and ceremonial arenas was common practice among the indigenous population of Gran Canaria, although Gáldar is without doubt

Fig. 4.7 Members of the
public watching the
panoramic audiovisual
display in the Cueva Pintada
de Gáldar Archaeological
Park and Museum (Gran
Canaria). Photograph: Javier
Betancor. ©Cabildo de Gran
Canaria

the most complex and best preserved example. It involved the use of mineral-based colors (ochres—highly oxidized clays—to produce red and pale clays for white). The motifs painted in this ceremonial area have been associated with ideograms that may be related to a system for measuring and calculating time, an elaborate lunar and solar calendar organized around a combination of series based on the number 12 and alternating between red, white, and unpainted spaces. This interpretation is reinforced by the findings inside the Cueva Pintada itself at the time when it was discovered (mummies, vessels, and other items).

• Visitor and Educational Tours

Tours of this urban archaeological park consist of visits to the polychrome chamber and to a recreated group of indigenous houses, which help the public to understand the ruins. Both the domestic items arranged inside the dwellings and the audiovisual equipment installed in them to contextualize and supplement their contents play an essential role in this process. Part of indigenous Gáldar is therefore transformed into a stage on which a museum project is presented, aiming essentially to take visitors on a journey into the past, combining stereoscopic and panoramic audiovisuals (Fig. 4.7), 3D computer graphics, display cases, panels, models, and reconstructions of indigenous dwellings.

A significant part of the museological discourse in Cueva Pintada revolves around the figure of Arminda (Rodríguez and Correa 2011), an historical figure who lived in this indigenous settlement in the late fifteenth century. The girl, who was the daughter of the last *Guanarteme* (chief) of the island, witnessed the final moments of the Canarian indigenous culture and the complex colonization of the island after the Castilian victory in the Canary Islands War. The character has also become the star of the activities prepared for children and families, which include stories, puppet shows, and workshops. The project is the result of interdisciplinary teamwork in which professionals from the various fields of history, archaeology, museology, teaching, literature, media, music, the visual and performing arts, and sociocultural entertainment, among others,have transformed Arminda into the most faithful ally of Cueva Pintada. However, the project is not just about learning more about Cueva Pintada and one of the most exciting periods in the history of the Island. It is also about encouraging participation, reflection, communication, and inclusion, in an effort to make historical heritage a primary resource for social cohesion. Arminda's synergy is therefore essential to conveying the contents of the museum and in particular to perpetuating a magical atmosphere that transcends the barrier of time, creating a space in which people can share, reflect on, and enjoy history.

Between July 2006 and August 2007 the Gáldar museum and archaeological park received 75,091 visitors. This makes it one of the most popular museums in the Canary Islands and also ranks it among the most widely visited museums in Spain, with figures comparable to those recorded for the best archaeological sites in Europe. The majority of visitors, moreover (55%), are local people from the Canary Islands.

4.7.2   Belmaco and La Zarza y La Zarcita (La Palma)

In the case of the island of La Palma, the Cueva de Belmaco (Mazo) has been a leading reference for the indigenous past of the island since the eighteenth century. The cave became famous at the time for its rock engravings and was associated with the residence of the local chiefs of Tigalate, Juguiro, and Garehagua. José de Viera y Clavijo was the first author to mention the site in the first volume of his *Historia General de las Islas Canarias* (1772), followed by authors such as René Verneau, Sabin Berthelot, Karl von Fritchz, and Gregorio Chil y Naranjo in the nineteenth century. There was a considerable increase in references and studies of the site throughout the twentieth century, to the point where it became one of the most widely cited archaeological zones in the Canary Islands (Hernández 1999; Farrujia 2009).

The La Zarza y La Zarcita rock complex (Garafía) was discovered much later, and it was not until 1941 that Elías Serra y Avelina Mata published the results of his findings in the *Revista de Historia*. This discovery unquestionably opened up a new phase in research into rock art in La Palma, with the inventory for the island increasing from that time onwards. In the case of both the Cueva de Belmaco and La Zarza y la Zarcita, the sites were quickly used in many publications as archaeological arguments for relating the indigenous population of the Canary Islands to the Atlantic context, to the Bronze Age (Farrujia 2004).

• The Belmaco (Mazo) Archaeological Park

The Cueva de Belmaco (Fig. 4.8) stands 390 m above sea level and is large (35 m wide, with a maximum height of approximately 10 m). Famous for its rock engravings and, to a lesser extent, as a dwelling place, it is located in an archaeological zone that includes other indigenous sites (burial caves and cave dwellings). The fact that the cave contains engravings has led some authors to identify it as a possible sanctuary or cultural area. The four panels of engravings, executed on large rocks that form part of the site have been displaced from their original location. They display wavy, spiral, and coiled shapes and circular and semi-circular motifs were created using the pecking technique. The motifs are similar to those documented in other rock art sites on the island.

Fig. 4.8 The Belmaco Cave
(Mazo, La Palma)

Fig. 4.9 The Visitor Centre at
the Belmaco Archaeological
Park. Detail of a display case
containing replicas of ceramic
vessels from the different
phases documented at the site

Several excavations carried out at the site revealed a complex stratigraphy, on the basis of which separate ceramic phases have been defined (Hernández 1999) during the research period when ceramics were considered the cultural element that could determine the chronology, origins, and relations between particular human groups (Farrujia 2004). The first of these phases is associated with an early settlement on the island in around the third century BC. The fact that the cave was in use up to the 1950s also gives it ethnographic value. An oven and a stone pavement, once part of a barn, have been preserved in the interior.

The site was declared an archaeological zone BIC on March 14th, 1986 (Decree 49/1986), and the archaeological park (Figs. 4.9 and 4.10) opened on March 25th, 1999. The park has a Museum or Interpretation Centre displaying various material items from the indigenous world of La Palma. In 2008 it received 15,114 visitors, most of whom were members of the local Canarian public.

• The La Zarza y La Zarcita Cultural Park (Garafía)

This archaeological complex consists of shepherd's settlements, various seasonal cave dwellings, and five rock engraving sites: La Zarza, La Zarcita, Llano de la Zarza, Fuente de Las Palomas, and Fajaneta del Jarito, although the best-known and most interesting are the first two, which have been the subject of archaeological interventions. La Zarza is one of the most complex and scientifically interesting sites

Fig. 4.10 The Visitor Centre
at the Belmaco
Archaeological Park. Detail
of a display case containing
replicas of ceramic vessels
and a replica of the main rock
art motif found at the site

in La Palma, due to the amount of engraved surfaces (29 panels) and the complexity
and broad chronology of the engraved motifs. In addition, it includes various shelters
that were excavated at the end of the 1990s. La Zarcita is smaller in size (18 panels)
and chronology and is distinctive with regard to the contrast between its engravings
(basically waving shapes) and those of La Zarza (which have more iconographic
variety), particularly given the short distance between the sites, although both stand
1,000 m above sea level.

The rock motifs (Fig. 4.11) may be divided into four basic categories: spiral,
circular, wavy, and linear, appearing alone or in groups, and were executed using the
pecking technique and abrasion. They are usually interpreted as a magical practice
to create favorable natural conditions associated with water, because the spirals and
waving lines are related to symbolic representations of water (a vital element) and
also with moon cults, with the aim of ensuring plentiful natural resources as a basis for
productive strategies (Martín 1998). From a material point of view, the excavations
that took place at the site have revealed significant amounts of ceramics that have

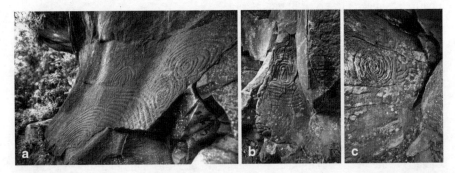

Fig. 4.11 Different panels containing rock art motifs. La Zarza y La Zarcita Cultural Park (Garafía,
La Palma). Photograph: Tarek Ode

Fig. 4.12 View of the Visitor Centre at the La Zarza y La Zarcita Cultural Park (Garafía, La Palma)

enabled a chronology to be established, in which the first occupation, as in the case of Belmaco, can be identified as being around the turn of the third century BC.

The importance of the site led to it being declared an Asset of Cultural Interest, within the archaeological zone category in 1986, and in 1998 it was made into the first archaeological park in the Canary Islands (Fig. 4.12), as a result of the collaboration among the Canarian Directorate-General for Historical Heritage, the La Palma council, and the Garafía local council.

The quantity, variety, and quality of rock art finds in La Palma have increased in recent years, following the various archaeological campaigns developed on the island. It currently has around 300 sites, approximately 900 panels and over 11,000 rock engravings which, given its area, means that the island has one of the largest concentrations of rock engravings per square meter on the planet. In terms of heritage, La Palma is therefore on a level with other geographical areas containing rock art sites that are inscribed in the World Heritage List, such as Algeria (Tassili n'Ajjer 1982) and Libya (Tadrart Acacus 1985) in Africa; Spain (Cueva de Altamira 1985 and Arco Mediterráneo 1998), France (Vallée de la Vézère caves 1979), Italy (Val Camonica 1979), Norway (Alta 1985), and Sweden (Tanum 1994) in Europe; Australia (Kakadú National Park 1981–1987–1992), Brazil (Parque Nacional de la Sierra de Capibara, 1991), and Mexico (Sierra de San Francisco, 1993).

In April 1995 an application was submitted to UNESCO for the La Palma engravings to be declared a World Heritage Site. Just over a decade later, in 2009, the La Palma council planned to launch a new and more ambitious project that would cover the rest of the Canary Islands, with the aim of enhancing the archaeological treasures of the islands through an application to UNESCO to declare the rock engravings and archaeological sites a World Heritage Site. The project would form part of a kind of tourism and cultural network that would include the indigenous Canarian heritage. Within this framework, a Canarian Historic Centres Network would be created that would include the so-called Canarian Archaeology Routes, promoted in collaboration with the government of the Canary Islands. However, the initiative, which included the local and island councils backed by the International Centre for Heritage Conservation (CICOP), which has its headquarters in La Laguna, has not been successful.

In relation to this proposal, the La Palma council is currently planning to open two more archaeological parks on the island at Cueva del Tendal (San Andrés y Sauces) and El Roque de Los Guerra (Villa de Mazo), in addition to the La Palma Archaeological Museum (Los Llanos de Aridane) opened in 2007, a modern building equipped with the latest audiovisual and museum resources to provide information on the indigenous past of the island.

4.7.3   El Júlan (El Hierro)

The rock engravings at El Julan (Frontera, El Hierro) were discovered in 1873 by Aquilino Padrón, who recognized that they were alphabetic from the outset, defining them as "possible early written symbols" (Padrón 1874).[17] The engravings were soon studied by various French authors including Sabin Berthelot, Louis Leon Cesar Faidherbe, and René Verneau who, influenced by the North African frame of reference and above all by the methodology developed by French archaeology in the Maghreb, classified them as Numidian or Libyan hieroglyphic inscriptions which had clear parallels in North Africa. Since then, the El Julan engravings have occupied a central place in archaeological literature on the sequencing for the indigenous population of the Canary Islands produced since the end of the nineteenth century (Hernández 2002; Farrujia 2009).

The site forms part of the El Julan Archaeological Zone, declared a BIC in 1985 and currently part of the Frontera Rural Park.[18] It opened to the public in July 2008, as part of the Interpretation Centre in the El Julan Cultural Park. The rock art site consists of two lava outflows and the engravings are found on their edges. The first group, Los Letreros, is larger and its panels are bigger and more complex. It consists of 69 panels containing engravings. This set stands near a *tagoror*, a dry stone structure used by the indigenous people as a place for holding council meetings (Fig. 4.13). The second group, Los Números, lies 500 m north of the former and consists of 37 panels (Hernández 2002). Another set of engravings, currently being studied, was identified recently in the same area of El Julan and may add meaning to this archaeological site.

The rock art motifs documented in El Julan, created using the pecking technique, include Lybico-Berber inscriptions (also documented in other sites on the island and on the rest of the Canary Islands) and, above all, geometrical engravings composed of isolated circles, intersected by one or more diameters or tangents, wavy lines, horseshoe-shaped motifs, and so on. These geometric motifs usually form

---

[17] The name "Júlan" comes from the plant known as *julan* or *julian* (ferula).

[18] The El Hierro Town and Country Planning Island Plan (Decree 132/95 of 11 May) recognizes it as a Historic Reserve. The land is owned by the government of the Canary Islands.

Fig. 4.13 *Tagoror* at El Julan (Frontera, El Hierro). Photograph: Tarek Ode

very complex panels, some of which are several meters wide, and have clear affinities with those documented in the African Atlas region. The sixth century BC has been suggested as the most likely period for the Lybico-Berber inscriptions in El Julan (Farrujia et al. 2010).

In the area surrounding the rock complexes, shells have also been recorded (large mounds of mollusc remains, resulting from the dietary practices of the indigenous societies), as well as sacrificial altars, cave dwellings, and burial caves. The sacrificial altars are oval or circular stone constructions interpreted as spaces dedicated to ritual practices (the sacrifice of goats, pigs, and sheep).

• The El Julan Cultural Park Interpretation Centre

The center has two floors dedicated to displays relating to the life of the indigenous populations of El Hierro and, in particular, the cultural evidence they left behind in El Julan, including the Tagoror, Los Letreros, and Los Números. It also provides accommodation for researchers.

The building, which stands 800 m above sea level, offers visitors spectacular views of the park, which has great landscape value and is located in the south of the island between Barranco de Garañones and La Dehesa Comunal (with a total area of around 55 hectares). It includes part of the Mar de Las Calmas and the entire La Restinga Marine Reserve and provides an opportunity to observe the different types of vegetation in the Canary Islands (Spanish juniper, pine, giant cactus, and *tabaibal*) and the main crops, as well as El Lajial, one of the areas in the Islands with the highest concentration of volcanic cones.

Various guided walks lead off from the center, showing the main evidence of the former way of life of the indigenous people of the islands. There are also very valuable ethnographic displays, because the El Julan caves were used by shepherds in past times.

The El Julan site (Fig. 4.14) is currently one of the places most frequently visited in El Hierro, according to information provided by the council staff responsible for its management. An average of 30 people per day visit the site, "whereas before there would be only three or four a day," according to one staff member. In winter, the visitors are mainly European, in particular Germans, and they are well informed about the importance of the park's heritage, whereas in summer the visitors are usually Canarian tourists staying in El Hierro who have heard about the park. In fact, they often visit the Interpretation Centre first and return the next day for the guided walk.

4.8   The Current Trend in Archaeological Heritage Management in the Canary Islands

The sites that have been analyzed in the previous pages, namely la Cueva Pintada de Gáldar (Gran Canaria), La Zarza, La Zarcita, and Belmaco (La Palma), and El Julan (El Hierro), are examples of archaeological parks in which value is placed on the indigenous Canarian heritage. In the specific case of Gran Canaria, there are also a number of other different archaeological sites that can be visited and enjoyed by the public. These include the sites at El Cenobio de Valerón (a communal silo in Santa María de Guía), Cuatro Puertas (cave dwellings, engravings, and an *almogaren* or place of worship, in Telde), Poblado de Tufia (dry stone houses in Telde), and Bentayga (an *almogaren* in the Montaña de Tejeda, associated with caves that have been excavated, a barn, and rock art). They do not have Interpretation Centres, but do offer information panels in which the main features of the archaeological sites are explained.

In Tenerife, La Gomera, and Lanzarote there are no archaeological parks or sites suitable for visitors. In Gran Canaria the situation is clearly in contrast, as in this island an active and comprehensive policy for heritage recovery has been developed. But in islands such as La Palma and El Hierro the heritage management policies have focused on recovering and valuing the indigenous sites that feature in the Canarian historiographic tradition as the result of archaeological work, and are directly related to rock "art" and the artistic and aesthetic elements implicit in this type of archaeological evidence. This is the case, for example, with the main archaeological parks in the Canary Islands: La Cueva Pintada de Gáldar, La Zarza, La Zarcita, La Cueva de Belmaco, and El Júlan.

Consequently, the recovery and valorization of the Canarian archaeological heritage is naturally undertaken on the basis of the actual significance that the sites have for our understanding of the indigenous world and the dissemination of this knowledge in present-day society, and also on the basis of: (a) values associated

Fig. 4.14 Different panels containing rock art motifs. El Julan Archaeological Park (Frontera, El Hierro). Photograph: Tarek Ode.

with memory, including the age and specific nature of the sites, as affirmed by archaeological interventions, as well as extrinsic historical values based on references to the sites in historiographic sources that lie outside the indigenous cultural tradition and are infused with a strong ethnocentric bias; (b) contemporary value, including artistic value per se, even though the rock evidence does not specifically constitute works of art, but may acquire an important meaning for society. In this sense, the actual concept of rock "art,"as pointed out by Chapa Brunet (2000), emerges from a focus originating in the background of the researchers themselves and does not reflect any similar concept in the ancient societies being studied.[19] In addition, these sites have occupied a key place in the different hypotheses relating to the indigenous population of the Canary Islands developed from the end of the nineteenth century up to the present day. The archaeological literature produced during this period offers no doubts in this respect (Farrujia 2004).

Therefore, among all the evidence relating to the indigenous Canarians, there are two examples that have historically attracted particular attention: the rock engravings and, as discussed in the previous chapter, mummification. In the case of the rock engravings, and in addition to their intrinsic aesthetic value, the following fact deserves consideration: both the Lybico-Berber and the Latin-Canarian rock inscriptions documented in the islands show that the indigenous populations were not illiterate. The Canary Islands was therefore the last bastion of the languages spoken in North Africa until the Arab conquest in the seventh century AD. However, most of the Canarian rock art and archaeological sites, in the broadest sense of the term, have no security or protection measures, a situation that is leading to irreparable loss of the indigenous Canarian heritage as a consequence of looting. The management of this heritage is defined on the basis of the following fundamental principles:

a. Concepts of shared or social memory have changed and fragmented in recent decades and this should be understood as a cultural effect of globalization that is particularly powerful in a fragmented territory (insular isolation) such as the Canarian archipelago.

b. Globalization is blurring local and regional identities. Therefore, in the recovery and management of the Canarian indigenous heritage, there has been a high degree of correspondence between the concepts of culture and identity that form part of a powerful, internationally recognized discourse of collective identity in the present, and those that inform our understanding of the past, shaping the description and classification of archaeological evidence as well as its interpretation. Naturally, this argument entails acceptance of the idea already stated in the opening lines of this chapter: the production of archaeological knowledge is contingent not only on the political interests and background of the individual practitioners, but also on the sociohistorical origins of the very paradigms that are used to describe and interpret the past. The theories, concepts, and questions that we adopt influence the selection, description, and interpretation of particular

---

[19] A theoretical discussion of the use of the concept "art" to apply to rock evidence may be found in the work of Searight (2004) and Fraguas (2006).

"facts" (i.e., data are theory-laden), and these theories, concepts, and questions are, to some extent, a product of our own sociohistorical context.

c. The Amazighity of the Canarian archaeological heritage has no significant or appropriate role in academic discourse or in disseminating scientific knowledge to the general public, due to the failure to develop a deconstructed and decolonized archaeology of the Canary Islands. In this sense, the Amazigh cultural background is minimized in heritage interpretation in all the Canarian archaeological parks. This attitude, which reflects trends in Europe among other promoters of accepted national "high" cultures, has emerged: (a) in a context in which the modern Amazigh identity as an idea and, increasingly, as a movement serves as a tangible counterpoint to both state-dominated political and social life and opposition Islamist currents, as analyzed by Maddy-Weitzman (2012); (b) in a context in which Canarian demands of independence from Spain are postulated appealing to Amazigh roots.

d. The recovery of certain types of archaeological sites (rock art sites) has created an aesthetic of material memories and authenticity that is completely partial and fails to represent an integrated vision of the indigenous past. The aim is to make the indigenous past more like Europe by providing evidence of similar historical depth, represented in this case by precolonial "art."

e. The archaeological parks of El Julan, Belmaco, La Cueva Pintada, and La Zarza y La Zarcita are associated with significant events (as symbolic or sacred sites) and are seen as important symbols of the precolonial heritage of the archipelago. These parks also explicitly state the role of these remains in reinforcing a perception of the contemporary Canary Islands as a successful modern region, clearly establishing the "sacred" nature of these remains within the context of national/global heritage.

f. The definition of the Canarian indigenous past on the basis of the culture concept, as analyzed by Jones (2003), has invoked an inventory of cultural, linguistic, and material traits. Therefore, the resulting picture has been one of indigenous people with a "museum culture," uprooted from the deep historical field and devoid of dynamism and meaning. The consequences of such an approach are not restricted to academic studies and reports but, as already stated, are also evident in areas such as political policy, administrative practices, legislation, and heritage management. In this sense, the preservation of the Canarian indigenous heritage provides a typical example of this objectification of culture, whereby a body of static cultural characteristics becomes reified as an object possessed by the nation. The definition, inventory, and circumscribing of what is regarded as "authentic" indigenous culture is therefore embedded in a Western or globalized world view.

g. The cultural–historical framework still present in Canarian archaeology contributes to this objectification of culture, allowing for a reconstruction of the past in terms of the distribution of homogeneous cultures whose history unfolds in a coherent linear narrative, namely a narrative that is measured in terms of objectified events, such as contacts, migrations, and conquests, with intervals of homogeneous empty time between them. Thus, attempts to identify past cultural entities in Canarian archaeology have been particularly suited to the construction

of national traditions, which are concerned with establishing a legitimate continuity with the past, rather than with understanding historical discontinuities and
the evolution of social contradictions.

The enduring nature of this cultural–historical framework is due to history itself, as it has affected archaeology in Spain, the significance of the Franco
legacy, the delayed involvement in external debates, the institutionalization and
self-reproduction of key archaeologies, a lack of contact with other schools and
academic communities, the lack of theoretical literature translated into Spanish,
coupled with limited foreign language skills, and the structure of the academic
field in Spain, where cronyism prevails. As González Ruibal has noted (2012) in
this respect, succession rather than subversion strategies, in the terms of Pierre
Bourdieu, are usually the ones that ensure a position in many universities and research centers: in other words, those that echo rather than contradict the majority.
This means that reflecting on theory is not encouraged, inasmuch as reflection
leads to criticism.

h. Policies directed towards recovering the past differ from one island to another
   due to the different archaeological heritage management priorities in each island
   council, and this is leading to a distorted and fragmented vision of the indigenous
   past. This policy paves the way for the "Balkanization" of Canarian archaeology
   and the emergence of "indigenous island cultures" (Tejera 2006). Each council has
   favored the recovery of "its" particular indigenous past: each island would have
   been populated by a specific ethnic group with its own particular culture. However,
   archaeology does not support this fragmented and instrumentalist hypothesis for
   the indigenous past (Farrujia 2007).

There is, however, one unifying element: all the existing archaeological parks in the
Canary Islands are based on rock sites that have played a leading role in the Canarian
historiographic tradition and enable indigenous Canarian "artistic" creations to be
equated with European heritage values.

The indigenous Canarian heritage, with all the problems inherent to its interpretation and management, has not been fully incorporated into the tourism industry
in the Canary Islands, although tourism has been the main economic activity in the
islands since the 1960s (Hernández and Santana 2010). This is specifically analyzed
in the following section.

4.9   Archaeology and Tourism in the Canary Islands

The Canary Islands, together with Hawaii and the Balearic Islands, represent the three
major international archipelagos for sun and beach tourism. These three archipelagos may also be considered mature tourism destinations, following Butler's lifecycle
model: in addition to having achieved very high figures for tourism and maintaining an economic and territorial impact for several decades, they are also showing
symptoms of stagnation (in the Canary Islands since the beginning of the twenty-first
century, and in Hawaii since the 1990s). In the case of the Balearic Islands, although
there was still significant development prior to the start of the world economic crisis
in 2007, there is also evidence of stagnation (Corral and Hernández 2010).

In the specific case of the Canary Islands, the climate makes the islands unusual to a certain extent, because there are no marked differences between the seasons (with tourists visiting throughout the year) and the high season is in winter. The archipelago offers a variety of attractions. There are the geographical features, the climate, the extensive beaches, and a certain exoticism to the landscape. In addition, there is also an advantageous exchange rate for foreign visitors, a wide range of accommodation, an important hotel infrastructure, and greater access to European metropolitan areas thanks to developments in air travel and reduced travel costs due to the spread of charter flights (Domínguez 2007). From the point of view of World Heritage, the Canary Islands already have three World Heritage Sites on the World Heritage list, due to their natural and historical values. They are Garajonay National Park (with a laurel forest from the Tertiary period that has disappeared from mainland Europe due to climate change, but formerly covered much of the southern continent), the Teide National Park (containing the highest volcano in Spain, the highest point above sea level in the Atlantic islands, and the most widely visited national park in Spain in 2010), and the city of San Cristóbal de La Laguna, discussed in previous pages.

This has meant that the archipelago receives very large numbers of tourists every year. In 2009, for example, 11,136,793 tourists visited the Canary Islands (50% from the United Kingdom, 42% from Germany, and 8% from mainland Spain), a particularly high number given that the archipelago has a population of 1,915,540 inhabitants and an area of 7,447 square km. However, this influx is unevenly distributed, inasmuch as Lanzarote, Fuerteventura, Gran Canaria, and Tenerife are the islands that receive the largest number of tourists, whereas La Gomera and El Hiero only receive 6.9% between them (Hernández and Santana 2010).

The importance of tourism in the Canary Islands can also be seen in the following fact: it represents 30% of the gross domestic product (GDP) and employs 37% of the working population (Villar 2009). However, the leading role played by tourism has been developed on the islands exclusively on the basis of mass tourism, associated with sunshine and beaches, and without taking advantage of the specific cultural heritage (including the archaeological heritage) in order to compete with other emerging or traditional destinations (Chávez et al. 2006; Chávez and Pérez 2010). In addition, although the accommodation and tourist facilities only occupy 3% of the island territory, they have had a very significant impact on natural resources, which has led to the need to control the growth of tourism through various laws that have not, however, been implemented efficiently (Villar 2009).

As Hernández and Santana have shown (2010), the Canarian tourism model has become exhausted in the face of new formulas and management concepts developed by the tourism industry in recent years, in which both cultural and natural heritage have become more important in response to tourist demands. In the case of the Canary Islands (excluding the example of Gran Canaria) tourism has failed to value archaeology and has not developed management models for the sites as tourism resources. Therefore there is no policy for archaeological tourism and no genuine archaeological tourism: in short, the role of archaeology within the Canarian tourism industry has been nonexistent. This is explained, as already noted, by the actual tourism model that has been developed on the islands and by the emphasis that the

100 In Search of the Indigenous Culture of the Canary Islands (1975–2012)

Canarian public administration has placed on the elitist heritage to the detriment of the indigenous heritage. It offers very few examples of sites that can be visited, although these do attract a significant number of visitors (as noted in previous pages) even though the majority are local. In Europe and, by extension, the Canary Islands, the architectural and cultural legacy is the main attraction for tourists and consequently the civil authorities have promoted and favored this, as can be seen in the analysis of Aguere. Nevertheless, this heritage policy contradicts the actual concept of cultural tourism, which has been defined as "travel designed to experience the places and activities that authentically represent the stories and people of the past" (National Trust for Historic Preservation 2001). In a broader sense, this includes travel to archaeological and historical sites, parks, museums, and places of traditional or ethnic significance. It also includes travel to foreign countries to experience different cultures and explore their prehistoric and historic roots. In the case of archaeology, the motivating forces behind archaeological tourism are a passion for the past and an interest in learning about the ancient or historical cultures that inhabited the area being visited. "Archaeotourists" are also attracted by the exotic (and often difficult to access) nature of the locations in which many archaeological sites are found and often seek out unique experiences.

Archaeological tourism is a lucrative business and a thriving industry. Tour operators, national and local governments, and local communities share the revenue derived from tourism, including entrance costs and other related fees and taxes. Tourism supports local businesses (hotels, restaurants, local crafts, and souvenir stores) and provides numerous job opportunities, including the recruitment and training of guides and interpreters. And, of course, archaeological tourism also creates less quantifiable benefits, such as increasing awareness of an area that may otherwise have been underappreciated as a travel destination. Increased attention can translate into income as more travelers visit the area. National and international exposure of a site can also lead to greater investment in its upkeep and maintenance by local and national governments. Consequently, increasing attention on an area can strengthen local identity, as communities in the vicinity of the sites become involved and invest in the maintenance and upkeep of a site that directly benefits them. Thus, archaeological tourism is an opportunity for community and regional development (Pinter 2005; Shackel 2005).

However, tourism also poses risks to heritage. The cases of Aguere and the Tindaya Mountain, previously analyzed, are clear examples of how the tourism model developed in the Canary Islands subordinates heritage policies to economic interests, with all the consequences this implies. In the case of Aguere, the declaration of the city as a World Heritage Site has boosted the recovery and preservation of the elitist, urban, essentially European heritage, while failing to include the African-based indigenous heritage in the tourism offer. In the case of Tindaya, the commodification of heritage for tourism purposes has led to plans to construct a monumental architectural project in one of the most important indigenous sites in the Canarian archipelago, with all the harmful consequences that will ensue for the conservation of the archaeological zone itself. In both cases the growing numbers of visitors are used to justify the implementation of heritage policies that do not favor cultural diversity and offer a distorted and partial interpretation of the past history of the islands.

Archaeological heritage management in the Canary Islands therefore distances itself from the concept of sustainable archaeological tourism, because the indigenous heritage cannot be made into an efficient tourism resource until it is valued more by the public authorities. As Olukole has commented (2009) within an African context, the location, conservation, and preservation of the cultural and natural resources of archaeological sites are of paramount importance to the success of a given area in attracting cultural heritage tourism. The cases of Aguere and the Tindaya Mountain represent the exact antithesis of this heritage management model.

Within the framework of this heritage policy, another situation should be recognized that is hindering the development of archaeological tourism in the Canary Islands: the Canarian Tourism and Culture Boards operate independently of each other, which explains the lack of joint policies for tourism. It is therefore imperative that efforts are made for the organizations and tourism and culture teams to work together, inasmuch as archaeological tourism initiatives cannot be developed in isolation. This administrative barrier is made worse by the geographical situation of the archipelago because, as previously noted, insularity has meant that the archaeological heritage in the Canary Islands has been treated differently in each of the islands. In the same way, the tourism image and offer in each island, the actual dynamics and nature of the archaeological work, and the institutional and administrative development of the political bodies that manage this type of heritage are different, because there is no common project that sees these resources as offering potential within cultural tourism and, more specifically, archaeological tourism.[20]

As analyzed in previous pages, there are very few archaeological sites in the Canary Islands that can be visited, and the majority are concentrated in one island, Gran Canaria, which is also the only island that has genuinely incorporated the archaeological heritage into its tourism business.[21] Moreover, it is difficult to access

---

[20] The Canarian Plan for the Restoration and Conservation of the Historical Heritage (2000–2010) is currently being implemented in the Canary Islands, with the main objective of conserving the historical heritage of the Islands. The policy framework for the (regional) plan, which covers the whole archipelago and therefore overcomes the intrainsular situation, contains numerous measures for the Canarian archaeological heritage, some of which have already been implemented, such as the Cueva Pintada de Gáldar Archaeological Park and the La Gomera and La Palma Archaeological Museums. In addition, the Arqueomac transnational cooperation project, a Canary Islands government culture initiative from the Directorate-General for Cooperation and Cultural Heritage, aims to promote cooperation projects and technological and scientific transfers in the field of archaeology. Since 2010, four meetings have been held in the islands of Fuerteventura, El Hierro, the Azores, and Madeira, as well as a series of e-learning training courses, together with the publication of two books of abstracts and the presentation and development of the Macronesia geographical–archaeological information system (SIGAMAC). The problematic of archaeology and tourism in the Canary Islands has been one of the themes covered within the Arqueomac project.

[21] Evidence of this can be seen in the promotion of some of its most important sites at international tourism fairs. In addition, the Gran Canaria Island Council, through the Culture and Historical Heritage Board, has made efforts to publicize them among the islanders through guided tours conducted by specialists. It has also published a guide to the archaeological heritage of Gran Canaria that indicates which sites can be visited, how to get to them, and so on (Velasco et al. 2001) and is involved in important information and awareness-raising measures through initiatives such as "Heritage for all" (http://www.estodotuyo.com), the information program "Heritage: open to

the majority of the sites that are not open to visitors, in terms of factors such as the surrounding area and proximity to tourist centers. It should also be remembered that accessibility is seen as one of the criteria for evaluating a tourist site. Moreover, there are no incentives for tourists interested in archaeological tourism in the Canary Islands, basically because the definition and supply of the essential elements that would enable visitors to understand the indigenous Canarian world have been directed essentially to the local public.[22] As Binoy has noted (2011) in relation to this problem in his analysis of the Hindu case, or Merriman (2005) from a more general perspective, every heritage tourism destination is essentially in need of a sound heritage tourism policy to ensure its healthy and sustainable development. Having an effective and efficient heritage interpretation mechanism essentially ensures sustainable and responsible heritage tourism development in heritage destinations. The interpretation processes are therefore those that make the presentation and social use of heritage possible. However, this rule is not always followed, inasmuch as fantastic interpretations are offered in an effort to make sites more exciting or mysterious, although they are usually not supported by scientific research and may give visitors the wrong impression of a site. This is the case with the "Pirámides de Guimar" Ethnographic Park (Tenerife), where pyramids dating from the seventeenth century have been related to the indigenous past—without any scientific justification—in order to link Canarian prehistory to ancient Egypt and the culture of the Pharaohs, as well as the Mesoamerican pyramids (Aztecs), on the basis of ultradiffusionist theories, as analyzed by Molinero Polo (2006).

Another complex issue concerns the need for accessible archaeological sites to be specifically covered by the various regulations for museums, as well as in the State Law on Museums in cases in which management of these spaces cannot be transferred. In these developments specific legislation, as well as their own regulations, should reflect the need and obligation to follow strategic plans and accepted criteria for the valuation of archaeological sites. The accessible archaeological sites, which usually have infrastructures such as Interpretation Centres or small site museums, cannot be exclusively subjected to heritage legislation. An accessible site can be made into a museum institution from the moment it is ascribed value and educational content that extends beyond mere scientific interest. Therefore, in accordance with the principles developed in other countries, this type of place has to be taken into specific consideration in legislation on museums, as previously noted, otherwise infrastructure will develop on the fringes of the law, with all the lack of support and control that this implies. Legislation on tourism should also address and categorize these new resources.

The situation in the Canary Islands described here in relation to archaeological tourism does not differ greatly from the situation in the rest of Spanish territory,

---

all" and "Jonah and archaeology" (http://www.jonasyelpatrimonio.com). The Tourist Board offers a series of themed routes for discovering the archaeological heritage of the island.

[22] Even the few publications that have covered the subject of archaeological tourism in the Canary Islands (Chávez and Pérez 2010; and Chávez et al. 2006) suffer from evident localism by failing to take the international frame of reference into account in their analysis.

because there is also a great divide between archaeology and the tourism industry in the majority of autonomous communities (Morère and Jiménez 2007; Verdugo and Parodi 2012). Nevertheless, there are some exceptions in mainland Spain, in areas such as Cantabria, where archaeology is an established tourism imitative and destination. Andalusia, Murcia, Galicia, Castile, and León still lag behind but are becoming communities in which the bid for archaeological tourism is becoming established. They are presented as archaeological tourism destinations with a certain value and, as such, are open to public and private investment. The Valencian community, in turn, is an established "sun and beach" destination but at the same time is one of the autonomous communities with the largest number of archaeological museum facilities, sometimes associated with accessible sites (Verdugo and Parodi 2012).

In Spain, in short, archaeological tourism is an emerging market that is poorly understood and, in general, badly structured, lacking specific legal or regulatory support and rarely associated with strategic plans. This differs enormously from the situation in other areas such as the United States (Hoffman et al. 2002) or India (Kumar 2009; Binoy 2011), where cultural tourism offers many potential benefits, in particular for the communities in which archaeological parks are located.

References

Álvarez Delgado, J. (1944–1945). La necrópolis guanche del Becerril. Informes y Memorias de la Comisaría General de Excavaciones Arqueológicas, Vol. 14. Excavaciones arqueológicas en Tenerife, Canarias. Plan Nacional, 1944–1945. Madrid: Comisaría General de Excavaciones. Ministerio de Educación Nacional.

Atalay, S. (2006). Indigenous archaeology as decolonizing practice. *American Indian Quarterly, 30*(3/4), 280–310. [Special Issue: Decolonizing Archaeology (Summer—Autumn)].

Bhabha, H. (1994). *The location of culture.* New York: Routledge.

Binoy, T. A. (2011). Archaeological and heritage tourism interpretation. A study. *South Asian Journal of Tourism and Heritage, 4*(I), 100–105.

Blair, P. J. (2005). The non-protection of Canadian aboriginal heritage (burial sites and artifacts). The Scow Institute, October. www.scowinstitute.ca. Accessed 14 Apr 2012.

Burchac, M. M., Hart, S. M., & Wobst, H. M. (Eds.). (2010). *Indigenous archaeologies: A reader on decolonization.* Walnut Creek: Left Coast Press.

Carlson, K., & McHalsie, A. J. (2010). *The power of place, the problem of time: Aboriginal identity and historical consciousness in the cauldron of colonialism.* Toronto: University of Toronto Press.

Cleere, H. (Ed). (1984). *Approaches to the archaeological heritage.* Cambridge: Cambridge University Press.

Cleere, H. (Ed). (2000). *Archaeological heritage management in the modern world. One world archaeology* (Vol. 9). New Cork: Routledge.

Corral, S., & Hernández, J. (2010). El turismo en destinos maduros archipielágicos: condicionantes y estrategias. El caso de los tres grandes: Hawai, Canarias y Baleares. In R. Hernández Martín & A. Santana Talavera (Eds.), *Destinos turísticos maduros ante el cambio. Reflexiones desde Canarias* (pp. 233–254). La Laguna: Instituto Universitario de Ciencias Políticas y Sociales.

Chafik, M. (2005). Treinta y tres siglos de la Historia de los Imazighen (Bereberes). Rabat (Morocco): Institut Royal de la Culture Amazighe. Centre de la Traduction, de la Documentation de l'Edition et de la Communication.

Chapa Brunet, T. (2000). Nuevas tendencias en el estudio del Arte Prehistórico. Arqueoweb, 2(3). http://www.ucm.es/info/arqueoweb. Accessed 21 Jun 2011.

Chávez Álvarez, M. E., Pérez González, E., Pérez Caamaño, F., Soler Segura, J., & Tejera Gaspar, A. (2006). La gestión del Patrimonio Arqueológico y el turismo en las Islas Canarias (España). Actas del II Congreso Internacional de Turismo Arqueológico. Barcelona: Universitat de Barcelona. http://www.academia.edu/2240546/La_gestion_del_Patrimonio_arqueologico_y_el_Turismo_en_las_Islas_Canarias_Espana_. Accessed 12 May 2012.

Chávez Álvarez, M. E., & Pérez González, E. M. (2010). La gestión e interpretación del patrimonio arqueológico. Nuevos modelos para el desarrollo turístico en Canarias. In R. Hernández Martín & A. Santana Talavera (Eds.), Destinos turísticos maduros ante el cambio. Reflexiones desde Canarias (pp. 49–70). La Laguna (Spain): Instituto Universitario de Ciencias Políticas y Sociales.

Chatterjee, P. (1993). The nation and its fragments: Colonial and postcolonial histories. Princeton: Princeton University Press.

De Certeau, M. (2008). Andar en la ciudad (Marches dans la ville). Bifurcaciones. Revista de Estudios culturales urbanos. Número 7/ julio. www.bifurcaciones.cl. Accessed 17 Mar 2012.

Díaz-Andreu, M. (2012). Archaeological encounters: Building networks of Spanish and British archaeologists in the 20th century. Cambridge: Cambridge Scholars Publishing.

Diego Cuscoy, L. (2008 [1968]). Los Guanches. Vida y cultura del primitivo habitante de Tenerife. Santa Cruz de Tenerife: Instituto de Estudios Canarios.

Dietler, M. (2010). Archæologies of colonialism: Consumption, entanglement, and violence in ancient Mediterranean France. California: University of California press.

Disko, S. (2010). World heritage sites in indigenous peoples' territories: Ways of ensuring respect for indigenous cultures, values and human rights. In D. Offenhäußer, W. Ch. Zimmerli, & M. T. Albert (Eds.), World heritage and cultural diversity (pp. 167–177). Brandenburg: German Comission for UNESCO.

Domínguez Mújica, J. (2007). La cartografía en la promoción turística de Canarias (1880–1970). Boletín de la Asociación de Geógrafos Españoles, 44, 279–300.

El-Aissati, A. (2005). A socio-historical perspective on the Amazigh (Berber) cultural movement in North Africa. Afrika Focus, 18(1–2), 59–72.

Esposito, A., & Gaulis I. (2010). The cultural heritages of Asia and Europe: Global challenges and local initiatives. Rapporteurs' Report of the Roundtable. http://www.asef.org/images/docs/HeritageRoundtable-RapporteursReport.pdf. Accessed 15 July 2012.

Farrujia de la Rosa, A. J. (2003). The Canary Islands under Franco's dictatorship: Archaeology, national unity and African aspirations. Journal of Iberian Archaeology, 5, 209–222.

Farrujia de la Rosa, A. J. (2004). Ab Initio (1342–1969). Análisis historiográfico y arqueológico del primitivo poblamiento de Canarias. Col. Árbol de la Ciencia (Vol. 2). Sevilla: Artemisa Ediciones.

Farrujia de la Rosa, A. J. (2007). Arqueología y franquismo en Canarias. Política, poblamiento e identidad (1939–1969). Colección Canarias Arqueológica (Vol. 2). Santa Cruz de Tenerife (Spain): Organismo Autónomo de Museos y Centros. Cabildo de Tenerife.

Farrujia de la Rosa, A. J. (2008). Archaeology, politics and identity: the case of the Canary Islands in the 19th century. In N. Schlanger & J. Nordbladh (Eds.), Archives, ancestors, practices. Archaeology in the light of its history (pp. 247–259). New York-Oxford: AREA. INHA. Berghahn Books.

Farrujia de la Rosa, A. J. (2009). A history of research into Canarian rock art: Opening up new thoughts. Oxford Journal of Archaeology, 28(3), 211–226, (August).

Farrujia de la Rosa, A. J. (2010). En busca del pasado guanche. Historia de la Arqueología en Canarias (1868–1968). Santa Cruz de Tenerife (Spain): Edicion Ka.

Farrujia de la Rosa, A. J. (2011). Waiving the ancestors voices?" In N. Bicho (Ed.), IV Congreso de Arqueología Peninsular. Universidad de Algarbe. Faro, 14–19 de septiembre de 2004 (pp. 251–260). Lisbon: Ed. Universidade Do Algarbe.

Farrujia de la Rosa, A. J. (2012). ¿¿:Patrimonio Arqueológico, Patrimonio Mundial? En busca de la cultura Guanche en Aguere. In A. Castillo (Ed.), *Actas del Primer Congreso Internacional de Buenas Prácticas en Patrimonio Mundial: Arqueología. Menorca, 9–13 de abril de 2012* (pp. 247–259). Madrid: Editora Complutense. https://portal.ucm.es/web/publicaciones/congresos. Accessed 11 Jan 2013.

Farrujia de la Rosa, A. J., & García Marín, G (2005). The Canary Islands and the Sahara: Reviewing an archaeological problem. *Sahara, 16*, 55–62.

Farrujia de la Rosa, A. J., Pichler, W., Rodrigue, A., & García Marín, S. (2010). The Lybico-Berber and Latino-Canarian Scripts and the colonization of the Canary Islands. *African Archaeological Review, 27*(1), 13–41.

Ferguson, T. J. (1996). Native Americans and the practice of archaeology. *Annual Review of Anthropology, 25*, 63–79. www.anthro.annualreviews.org. Accessed 11 May 2013.

Forbes, N., Page, R., & Pérez, G. (Eds.). (2009). *Europe's deadly century. Perspectives on 20th century conflict heritage*. Belgium: English Heritage.

Foucault, M. (1977). L'oeil du pouvoir. In J. Benhtam (Ed.), *Le Panoptique* (pp. 13–26). Paris: Belfond.

Fraguas Bravo, A. (2006). De la hegemonía al panel. Una aproximación a la ideología del arte prehistórico del noreste africano. *Complutum, 17*, 25–43.

García Fernández, J. (Ed.). (1987). *Legislación sobre Patrimonio Histórico*. Madrid: Editorial Tecnos.

Giráldez Macía, J. (2007). Tindaya: el poder contra el mito. Málaga: Libre Ando ediciones. Zambra iniciativas sociales.

González Ruibal, A. (2010). Colonialism and European archaeology. In J. Lydon & U. Rizvi (Eds.), *Handbook of postcolonial archaeology* (pp. 37–47). Walnut Creek, California: Left Coast Press.

González Ruibal, A. (2012). Cada vez más islas. *Revista Arkeogazte, 2*, 17–19. www.arkeogazte.org/arkeogazterevista. Accessed 11 Jan 2013.

Gosden, C. (2001). Postcolonial archaeology: Issues of culture, identity and knowledge. In I. Hodder (Ed.), *Archaeological theory today* (pp. 241–61). Cambridge: Polity Press.

Gosden, Ch. (2004). *Archaeology and colonialism: Cultural contact from 5000 BC to the present*. Cambridge: Cambridge University Press.

Hachid, M. (2000). Les premiers berberes: entre Mediterranee, Tassili et Nil.Aix-en-Provence: Edisud.

Harrison, R. (2012). *Heritage. Critical approaches*. London-New York: Routledge.

Hartog, F. (2004). Tiempo y Patrimonio (Temps et histoire). *Museum International, 227*, 4–15.

Hernández Gómez, C. M., Alberto, V., & Velasco, J. (2004–2005). Enfoques y desenfoques en la arqueología canaria a inicios del siglo XXI. *Revista Atlántica-Mediterránea de Prehistoria y Arqueología Social, 7*, 175–188.

Hernández Martín, R., & Santana Talavera, A. (Eds.). (2010). *Destinos turísticos maduros ante el cambio. Reflexiones desde Canarias*. La Laguna: Instituto Universitario de Ciencias Políticas y Sociales.

Hernández Pérez, M. (1999). *La cueva de Belmaco. Mazo Isla de La Palma. Estudios Prehispánicos (Vol. 7)*. Madrid: Dirección General de Patrimonio Histórico.

Hernández Pérez, M. (2002). El Julan (La Frontera, El Hierro, Islas Canarias). Estudios Prehispánicos. Vol. 10. Madrid: Dirección General de Patrimonio Histórico. Viceconsejería de Cultura y Deportes del Gobierno de Canarias.

Hernández Pérez, M., Martín Socas, D. (1980). Nueva aportación a la prehistoria de Fuerteventura. Los grabados rupestres de la Montaña de Tindaya. Revista de Historia Canaria, XXXVII, pp. 13–41.

Hodder, I. (Ed.). (2001). *Archaeological theory today*. Cambridge: Polity Press.

Hoffman, T. L., Kwas, M. L., & Silvermann, H. (2002). Heritage tourism and public archaeology. *The SAA Archaeological Record*, March, pp. 30–32.

ICOMOS. (2005). *The world heritage list: Filling the gaps. An action plan for the future*. Paris: ICOMOS.

Ireland, T. (2002). Giving value to the Australian historic past: Archaeology, heritage and nationalism. *Australasian Historical Archaeology, 20*, 15–25.

Ireland, T. (2010). *Excavating globalization from the ruins of colonialism: Archaeological heritage management responses to cultural change.* ICOMOS Scientific Symposium Changing World, changing views of heritage: The impact of global change on cultural heritage. http://www.international.icomos.org/adcom/dublin2010/Paper_2.pdf. Accessed 15 Jan 2013.

Jay Stottman, M. (2010). *Archaeologists as activists. Can archaeology change the world? Alabama.* Alabama: University of Alabama Press. Tuscaloosa.

Jones, S. (2003). The archaeology of ethnicity. Constructing identities in the past and present. Taylor & Francis e-Library. http://www.karant.pilsnerpubs.net/files/Jones.pdf. Accessed 18 Sept 2012.

Kumar Patnaik, S. (2009). Archaeological heritage and tourism. *Orissa Review*, December, pp. 1–5.

Liebmann, M., & Rizvi, U. Z. (2010). *Archaeology and the poscolonial critique.* Plymouth : Altamira Press.

Lozny, L. R. (Ed.). (2011). *Comparative archaeologies: A sociological view of the science of the past.* Berlin: Springer.

Lydon, J., & Rizvi, U. (Eds.). (2010). *Handbook of postcolonial archaeology.* Walnut Creek: Left Coast Press.

Lyons, C. L., Papadopoulos, J. K. (Eds.). (2002). *The archaeology of colonialism.* Los Angeles: Getty Research Institute.

Maddy-Weitzman, B. (2006). Ethno-politics and globalisation in North Africa: The Berber culture movement. *The Journal of North African Studies, 11*, 71–83.

Maddy-Weitzman, B. (2011). North Africa's democratic prospects. Foreign Policy Research Institute. E-Notes. www.fpri.org. Accessed 12 Jan 2012.

Maddy-Wietzman, B. (2012). *The Berber identity movement and the challenge to North African States.* Austin: University of Texas Press.

Marciniak, A. (2000). Protection and management of archaeological heritage: The importance and achievements of the European Association of archaeologists. *Archaeologia Polona, 38*, 205–214.

Marcuse, H. (2002). *One-Dimensional man: Studies in the ideology of advanced industrial society.* New York: Routledge.

Martín Rodríguez, E. (1998). *La Zarza: entre el cielo y la tierra. Estudios Prehispánicos (Vol. 6).* Madrid: Dirección General de Patrimonio Histórico.

Mauch Messenger, Ph., & Smith, G. (2010). *Cultural heritage management. A global perspective.* Florida: University Press of Florida.

Merriman, T. (2005). Heritage interpretation: Tourism cake, not icing. *The SAA Archaeological Record. May, 5*(3), 36–38.

Mestre Martí, M. (2012). San Cristóbal de la Laguna, La Habana Vieja y el Viejo San Juan: Urbanismo y Patrimonio Arqueológico en la recuperación de tres centros históricos de ciudades de ultramar. In A. Castillo (Ed.), *Actas del Primer Congreso Internacional de Buenas Prácticas en Patrimonio Mundial: Arqueología. Menorca, 9–13 de abril de 2012* (pp. 436–449). Madrid: Editora Complutense. https://portal.ucm.es/web/publicaciones/congresos. Accessed 29 Jan 2013.

Molinero Polo, M. A. (2006). Pirámides de Güimar, solsticios, masonería y Egipto Antiguo. Tabona. *Revista de prehistoria y de arqueología, 15*, 163–178.

Morère Molinero, N., & Jiménez Guijarro, J. (2007). Análisis del turismo arqueológico en España. Un estado de la cuestión. *Estudios Turísticos, 171*, 115–139.

Mulvaney, K., & Hicks, W. (2012). Murujuga Madness: World Heritage values disregarded. In A. Castillo (Ed.), *Actas del Primer Congreso Internacional de Buenas Prácticas en Patrimonio Mundial: Arqueología. Menorca, 9–13 de abril de 2012* (pp. 187–201). Madrid: Editora Complutense. https://portal.ucm.es/web/publicaciones/congresos. Accessed 29 Jan 2013.

Nalda, E. (2004). La Arqueología Mexicana y su Inserción en el Debate sobre Diversidad e Identidad. *Museum International, 227*, 29–38.

National Trust for Historic Preservation. (2001). Heritage tourism program. http://www.nthp.org/heritagetourism/index.html. Accessed 11 Mar 2013.

Navarro Segura, M. I. (1999). La Laguna 1500: la ciudad-república. Una utopía insular según las leyes de Platón. La Laguna (Spain): Excmo. Ayuntamiento de San Cristóbal de La Laguna.

Navarro Segura, M. I. (2002). La maldición de la pirámide. O la perversa traición al escultor Eduardo Chillida. *Basa*, 27, (pp. 112–133). Santa Cruz de Tenerife (Spain): Colegio Oficial de Arquitectos de Canarias.

Onrubia Pintado, J. (2003). La Isla de los Guanartemes. Territorio, sociedad y poder en la Gran Canaria indígena (siglos XIV-XV). Madrid: Ediciones del Cabildo de Gran Canaria.

Onrubia Pintado, J., Rodríguez Santana, C. G., Sáenz Sagasti J. I., & Antona del Val, V. (2007). El Museo y Parque Arqueológico Cueva Pintada (Gáldar, Gran Canaria): de manzana agrícola a parque arqueológico urbano. IV Congreso Internacional sobre musealización de xacementos arqueolóxicos. Conservación e presentación de yacementos arqueolóxicos no medio rural. Impacto social no territorio (pp. 183–190). Santiago de Compostela: Xunta de Galicia.

Olukole, T. O. (2009). Changing cultural landscapes and heritage tourism potentials of Ijaiye-Orile archaeoloical sites in Nigeria. The African Diaspora Archaeology Network, June. www.diaspora.uiuc.edu/news0609/news0609.html. Accessed 13 Apr 2011.

Padrón, A. (1874). Relación de unos letreros antiguos encontrados en la isla del Hierro. Las Palmas de Gran Canaria.

Pagán Jiménez, J. R. (2004). Is all archaeology at present a postcolonial one? Constructive answers from an eccentric point of view. *Journal of Social Archaeology*, *4*(2), 200–213. (www.sagepublications.com). Accessed 13 Apr 2011.

Patou-Mathis, M. (2011). *Le Sauvage et le Préhistorique, miroir de l'Homme occidental. De la malédiction de Cham à l'identité nationale*. Paris: Odile Jacob.

Pellicer Catalán, M. (1968–69). Panorama y perspectivas de la arqueología canaria. Revista de Historia, XXXII (157–164), pp. 291–302.

Perera Betancort, M. A. (1996). La Montaña de Tindaya: valor natural, valor cultural. Análisis legal. VII Jornadas de Estudios sobre Fuerteventura y Lanzarote. Lanzarote: Cabildos de Lanzarote y Fuerteventura.

Perera Betancort, M. A., Belmonte Avilés, J. A., Esteban, C., Tejera Gaspar, A. (1996). Tindaya: un estudio arqueoastronómico de la sociedad prehispánica de Fuerteventura. Tabona, pp. 165–196.

Pinter, T. L. (2005). Heritage tourism and archaeology: Critical issues. *The SAA Archaeological Record. May*, *5*(3), 9–11.

Querol Fernández, M. A. (2010). *Manual de gestión del patrimonio cultural*. Madrid: Akal.

Querol Fernández, M. A., & Castillo, A. (2012). Arqueología Preventiva y Patrimonio Mundial. El ejemplo españo como base para el cambio en el ejercicio de la gestión arqueológica. In A. Castillo (Ed.), *Actas del Primer Congreso Internacional de Buenas Prácticas en Patrimonio Mundial: Arqueología. Menorca, 9–13 de abril de 2012* (pp. 51–65). Madrid: Editora Complutense. www.portal.ucm.es/web/publicaciones/congresos. Accessed 2 Jan 2013.

Ramonet, I. (2010 [1995]). Pensamiento único y nuevos amos del mundo. In N. Chomsky, N. & I. Ramonet (Eds.), *Cómo nos venden la moto. Información, poder y concentración de medios* (pp. 49–88). Barcelona: Editorial Icaria.

Ribeiro Durham, E. (1998). Cultura, patrimonio, preservación. *Alteridades*, *8*(16), 131–136.

Rodríguez, C. G., & Correa, T. (2011). ¡Hola! Me llamo Arminda... ¿y tú? A global communication project for Gran Canaria's Archaeological Heritage". *AP Journal*, *1*, 5–27.

Rodríguez Yanez, J. M. (1997). La Laguna durante el Antiguo Régimen. Desde su fundación hasta finales del siglo XVII. In M. de Paz Sánchez & J. Castellano Gil (Eds.), La Laguna: 500 años de historia. Vol. I. La Laguna (Spain): Excmo. Ayuntamiento de San Cristóbal de La Laguna.

Ross, A. (1996). More than archaeology: New directions in cultural heritage management. *QAR*, *10*, 17–24.

Sabir, A. (2008). Las Canarias prehispánicas y el Norte de África. El ejemplo de Marruecos. Paralelismos lingüísticos y culturales. Rabat: Institut Royal de la Culture Amazighe.

Saco del Valle, A. O. (2001). Los parques arqueológicos y el paisaje como patrimonio. Arqueoweb, 3–1. http://www.ucm.es/info/arqueoweb/pdf/3–1/almudenaorejas.pdf. Accessed 12 Feb 2011.

Said, E. W. (1997 [1979]). *Orientalismo (Orientalism)*. Barcelona: Editorial De Bolsillo.

Searight, S. (2004). *The prehistoric rock art of Morocco. A study of its extensión, environment and meaning. BAR International Series, 1310*. Oxford: Archaeopress.

Shackel, P. A. (2005). Local identity, national memory, and heritage tourism. Creating a sense of place with archaeology. *The SAA Archaeological Record. May, 5*(3), 33–35.

Smith, L., & Waterton, E. (2009). *Heritage, communities and archaeology*. London: Duckworth Academic and Bristol Classical Press.

Spivak, G. C. (1985). Subaltern studies: Deconstructing historiography. In R. Guha (Ed.), *Subaltern Studies IV. Writings on South Asian History and Society* (pp. 330–363). Delhi: Oxford University Press.

Tejera Gaspar, A. (2006). Los libio-bereberes que poblaron las Islas Canarias en la Antigüedad. In A. Tejera Gaspar (Ed.), *Canarias y el África Antigua* (pp. 81–105). Santa Cruz de Tenerife (Spain): Centro de la Cultura Popular Canaria.

Tejera Gaspar, A., Jiménez González, J., & Allen, J. (2008). Las manifestaciones artísticas prehispánicas y su huella. Historia Cultural del Arte en Canarias. Vol. I. Santa Cruz de Tenerife (Spain): Gobierno de Canarias.

Trigger, B. (2006). A history of archaeological thought (2nd edn.). Cambridge: Cambridge University Press.

Velasco Vázquez, J., Martín Rodríguez, E., Alberto Barroso, V., Domínguez Gutiérrez, Juan C., & León Hernández, J. (2001). Guía del Patrimonio Arqueológico de Gran Canaria. Las Palmas de Gran Canaria: Cabildo de Gran Canaria.

Veracini, L. (2006). A prehistory of Australia's history wars: The evolution of aboriginal history during the 1970s and 1980s. *Australian Journal of Politics and History, 52*(3), 439–468.

Verdugo Santos, J., & Parodi Álvarez, M. J. (2012). La valorización del patrimonio en Andalucía. Nuevas tendencias y estrategias. In M. Zouak, J. Ramos Muñoz, D. Bernal, & B. Raissouni (Eds.), Arqueología y turismo en el círculo del Estrecho. Colección de Monografías del Museo Arqueológico de Tetuán (Vol. III, pp. 37–67). Cádiz: Servicio de Publicaciones de la Universidad de Cádiz. Dirección Regional de Cultura Tánger-Tetuán del Reino de Marruecos.

Villar Rojas, F. J. (2009). La política turística de Canarias. In M. Simancas Cruz (Ed.), El impacto de la crisis en la economía canaria. Claves para el futuro. Vol. I. Santa Cruz de Tenerife (Spain): Real Sociedad Económica de Amigos del País de Tenerife.

Wallerstein, I. (2003). *Impensar las ciencias sociales. Límites de los paradigmas decimonónicos (Unthinking Social Science: The limits of nineteenth-century paradigms)*. Mexico: Siglo XXI Editores.

Watkins, J. (2005). Through wary eyes: Indigenous perspectives on archaeology. *The Annual Review of Anthropology, 34*, 429–449. www.anthro.annualreviews.org. Accessed 29 Mar 2013.

Willems, J. H. W. (1998). Archaeology and heritage management in Europe. Trends and developments. *European Journal of Archaeology, 1*(3), 293–311.

Willems, J. H. W. (Ed.). (2007). *Quality management in archaeology*. Oxford: Oxbow Books Limited.

Willems, J. H. W. (2010). Laws, language, and learning. Managing archaeological heritage resources in Europe. In Ph. Mauch Messenger & G. Smith (Eds.), *Cultural heritage management. A global perspective* (pp. 212–229). Florida: University Press of Florida.

Willems, J. H. W. (2012). World heritage and global heritage: The tip of the iceberg. In A. Castillo (Ed.), Actas del Primer Congreso Internacional de Buenas Prácticas en Patrimonio Mundial: Arqueología. Menorca, 9–13 de abril de 2012 (pp. 36–50). Madrid: Editora Complutense. https://portal.ucm.es/web/publicaciones/congresos. Accessed 29 Jan 2013.

Chapter 5
Conclusions

In times of globalization, and given the global impact of commerce, politics, and environmental stress on culture, it is interesting to see what kind of impact these stress factors have had on Canarian archaeological heritage management. This book is therefore an attempt to compare the Canarian archaeology with "other archaeologies" in the sense that archaeologists from around the world may be able to learn about each other and their work while focusing on the case of the Canary Islands. Thus, an issue that may have been specifically local may become relevant elsewhere. After all, to paraphrase Tracy Ireland (2010), although archaeologists act locally, they often have an impact on a site or landscape that is a part of the global human heritage. Therefore, we all have the right to take part in this discussion.

In this sense, this thematic study is the first regional monograph to be written on the archaeological heritage of the Canary Islands within the context of: (a) deconstructing colonial discourse to show how the history and politics of the past still have an undue influence on the way in which the present-day archaeological heritage is interpreted and managed; (b) recognition of archaeological heritage sites in the Canary Islands, their regional and international significance, and the need for national and regional heritage conservation policies to protect and sustain these assets; and (c) identifying the gaps in the current understanding of particular kinds of Canarian archaeological landscapes, in order to establish priorities for further detailed studies.

The study also includes an overview of some of the archaeological parks in the Canary Islands (La Cueva Pintada de Galdar in Gran Canaria, El Julan in El Hierro, Belmaco and La Zarza y La Zarzita in La Palma) and the defining characteristics that account for their common features as well as their diversity. As such, the study is essentially introductory, serving as a broad analysis of archaeological landscapes based on the information that is available, rather than a detailed assessment of possible individual nominations for the World Heritage List.

The Atlantic Ocean area in which the Canary Islands are located, close to the North African coast, gave rise to traditional indigenous ways of life that were unique to the region and were expressed through particular settlements and monuments, as well as the intangible heritage of traditions, knowledge, stories, songs, music, and dance, although the latter progressively disappeared following the conquest and colonization of the Canary Islands and the subsequent ethnocide, as described in the

A. J. Farrujia de la Rosa, *An archaeology of the margins*,
SpringerBriefs in Archaeology, DOI 10.1007/978-1-4614-9396-9_5,
© The Author(s) 2014

Introduction. Nevertheless, the material heritage reflects the common origins of the indigenous Canary Island societies and the specific ways of life developed on each island. This material heritage also reflects a common background shared with the North African Amazigh culture in the Moroccan Atlas region, Tunisia, Algeria, and Libya.

With regard to the archaeological situation of this Amazigh culture in the Canary Islands, the "indigenous phase" in the archipelago covers the period from the mid-first millennium BC to the rediscovery of the islands by European navigators in the fourteenth century. However, from a chronological–regional point of view, if applied to the Canary Islands, the ICOMOS report on the World Heritage List (2005) mentioned in Chap. 3 would fail to recognize that there had been any substantial change in the indigenous cultures of the Canary Islands over time, or in their social formation and use of the landscape and its resources. Moreover, from a geographical point of view, the indigenous archaeological heritage of the Canary Islands would never fit within the definition of the cultural region of "Europe" used by UNESCO as a unit of analysis following the said ICOMOS report. Cultural regions do not necessarily correspond to political boundaries. It is therefore not possible to aim for a "balance" in the World Heritage List at the State Party or national level. Unfortunately, this limits the usefulness of the findings of this research for sites in the Canary Islands.

Given these limitations, it is a complex task to make "global" the knowledge about Canarian archaeological heritage. In addition, from the point of view of archaeological heritage management, there is an obvious invisibility associated with archaeology in many urban and nonurban contexts in the European Union (the Canary Islands included) and Latin America, as recently analyzed in the *First International Conference on Best Practices in World Heritage: Archaeology* (see Castillo 2012; and Farrujia 2012, for the Canarian case). UNESCO itself is aware of this problem and many others, such as the well-known territorial imbalances, which are both quantitative and qualitative and also affect archaeology. However, despite a global strategy, the development of practical and operational directives, the "demands" of management plans or multiple formal complaints, letters, and recommendations from advisory bodies such as ICOMOS, it is clear that in most places World Heritage lacks a well-defined management strategy.

At a time of financial crisis and economic recession in many parts of the world, research and the management of archaeological heritage resources are facing new challenges. In Western countries, the existing infrastructures and legislation are under scrutiny and in developing countries the wisdom of importing Western procedures and ethics is rightly being questioned. At the same time, archaeological resources are increasingly being exploited for their economic potential without regard for their sustainable preservation. The UNESCO World Heritage List was intended to promote the preservation and enjoyment of the most important natural and cultural forms of heritage on the planet. It is now fast losing all credibility due to political maneuvering and the deliberate inclusion by the World Heritage Committee of sites that do not meet the requirements, for reasons of prestige, tourism, and economic purposes (Willems 2012).

Within this context, this research has also drawn attention to the main deficiencies in archaeological heritage management in the Canary Islands, and therefore, on a regional level. The current scenario for Canarian archaeology described in this book clearly reflects the fact that there is insufficient relevant current data on the extent, condition, authenticity, and integrity of the indigenous archaeological heritage in the Canary Islands. Policies directed towards recovering the past differ from one island to another, due to the different archaeological heritage management priorities of each Island Council and this is creating a distorted and fragmented vision of the indigenous past.

Although recognizing that this has political implications as well as implications for resources, involving local Canary Island people in some aspects of documenting fieldwork would be highly appropriate for future studies on a local or subregional level. At present few people in the Canary Islands have any training in archaeological heritage, and their involvement in the development and production of cultural and archaeological landscape studies would therefore provide an opportunity to build up these skills within the region.

Moreover, the case of the Canary Islands is an example of how the regional administration has placed a special emphasis on the recovery and management of the historical heritage, persistently emphasizing its architectural dimensions, which are European in origin. It has favored a partial reading of the cultural resources in the archipelago by marginalizing the archaeological heritage that predates the conquest and is North African in origin, particularly in Tenerife, La Gomera, Lanzarote, and Fuerteventura. This model does not, therefore, favor cultural diversity or the preservation of the indigenous archaeological heritage: if there is no dissemination of the Amazigh heritage within the public sphere, there can be no social awareness of it either. It should be remembered, as Smith (2006 p. 307) has pointed out, that heritage is a cultural and social process: it is a process of remembering and memory making, of mediating cultural and social change, and of negotiating, creating, and re-creating values, meanings, understandings, and identity. Above all, heritage is an active, vibrant cultural process of creating bonds through shared experiences and acts of creation.

Within the context of the indigenous heritage and from the point of view of heritage management, the policies developed on a regional scale, with the exception of Gran Canaria, have led to the recovery of a particular type of indigenous site, namely rock art sites, which have been organized to be appreciated and enjoyed by the public as archaeological parks. This is the case with the La Cueva Pintada (Gran Canaria), Belmaco and La Zarza y La Zarcita (La Palma), and El Julan (El Hierro). Given this, Canarian archaeological heritage management should invest in a more comprehensive recovery of the indigenous past that values other different kinds and types of sites (settlements, burial complexes, etc).

The Canarian Public Administration should seriously consider the potential for archaeological sites to appear on their Tentative Lists and be nominated for inscription on the World Heritage List.[1] The sites discussed in this study may have the

---

[1] As already pointed out in Chap. 3, the Canary Islands already have three World Heritage Sites inscribed in the World Heritage List, but these are sites with natural and historical assets.

potential to be considered World Heritage Sites (in particular, those in Gran Canaria and La Palma), but this will require far more detailed research and fieldwork. All of them clearly reflect the North African Imazighen influences on the Canarian archaeological heritage, therefore representing evidence of a considerable interchange of human values during a particular period of time and in a specific cultural area (the Canary Islands).[2] In addition, they are evidence of the indigenous culture prior to the conquest and colonization of the Canary Islands in the fourteenth and fifteenth centuries, offering unique evidence of a lost cultural tradition. Moreover they are, in general, located in areas of great landscape value, therefore meeting many of the criteria for inclusion in the World Heritage List, as established in the "Convention Concerning the Protection of the World Cultural and Natural Heritage" approved by UNESCO in November 1972. However, as previously stated, the archaeological sites included in this study are only examples and represent only some of the many sites worthy of further investigation.

Although the World Heritage Committee strongly supports customary management when this sustains outstanding universal value, this kind of management needs to be formalized to the extent that the desired state of conservation and monitoring and feedback systems are in place and there is evidence of adequate legal protection. There is clearly a need for capacity building in the Canary Islands to achieve a satisfactory level of management and protection in order to optimize the success of future nominations. The cases of Aguere (Tenerife) and the Tindaya Mountain (Fuerteventura) discussed in Chap. 3 clearly reflect this lack of management and protection.

The current trend in archaeological heritage management in the Canary Islands therefore reflects how the indigenous heritage is underrepresented. Yet there is evidence of this not only within the context of the Canary Islands, but also in discussions on a wider geographical scale and in relation to the World Heritage List itself. "Elitist" heritage and data from Europe are overrepresented, but the indigenous heritage is rarely a focus. This is why the management of the archaeological heritage during the colonial and postcolonial era was also discussed in this study, providing several examples from the Canary Islands (Aguere in Tenerife, or the Tindaya Mountain in Fuerteventura, are illustrative in this respect, as evidence of the neglect of the indigenous archaeological heritage). Although it is not a current priority for the regional government, this form of management during the colonial and postcolonial era does reflect diverse and shared, but also controversial histories and values with regard to the indigenous Canarian heritage. Although many histories of the various Canarian archaeological sites have been published, there are very little data available about sites that reflect these colonial histories. In future it may be worthwhile considering a regional study of colonial and postcolonial "landscapes," as developed in Australia (Ireland 2002).

With regard to the recovery and management of the indigenous Canarian heritage, there has therefore been a high degree of correspondence between the concepts of culture and identity that form part of a powerful, internationally recognized discourse of collective identity in the present, and those that inform our understanding of the

---

[2] A serial nomination with other North African nations might be advantageous to all parties concerned.

past, shaping the description and classification of archaeological evidence as well as its interpretation. The recovery of certain types of archaeological sites (rock art sites) has created an aesthetic of material memories and authenticity that is entirely partial and does not represent an integrated vision of the indigenous past. Instead it aims to make the indigenous past more like Europe by providing evidence of similar historical depth, represented in this case by precolonial "art," as in the case of the El Julan, Belmaco, La Cueva Pintada, and La Zarza y La Zarcita Archaeological Parks.

Given the progressive disappearance of the Canarian indigenous world from the fourteenth century onwards, and therefore the fact that there is no indigenous archaeology in the archipelago, this monograph establishes links between Canarian archaeology and the indigenous archaeologies developed in other geographical contexts. This is because the societies that are the subject of the study, namely the indigenous Canarians, were not prehistoric populations from distant times, but human groups contemporary with European expansionism in the Atlantic from the fourteenth century onwards. The fact that the indigenous Canarian people survived until the seventeenth century ensured that part of the indigenous (ethnographic) heritage was preserved in written sources produced by Europeans, albeit with an obvious ethnocentric approach. This ethnographic information on the indigenous Canarian world "contaminated" and influenced the archaeological work that was carried out from the mid-nineteenth century onwards by European researchers, and naturally ended up by imposing a logic of colonial discourse, as argued in the preceding chapters. In this sense, Canarian archaeology shares the effects of colonial discourse with indigenous archaeologies, as well as the process of internationalization that began in the 1970s, and the fact that it is underrepresented on a regional and international scale and from a heritage perspective in the face of the hegemonic weight of an "elitist" heritage. Moreover, from a political and geographical point of view, Canarian archaeology is influenced by a framework very similar to those found in other colonial and postcolonial contexts that do have indigenous archaeologies: the Canary Islands is a geographical area politically controlled by a distant country, a vestige of a past empire, and a national (Spanish) territory in the African continent, with obvious geostrategic value.

This lack of any indigenous archaeology in the Canary Islands created by, and for, indigenous people therefore implies that the contemporary interpretation of their legacy must be based on an external cultural horizon outside the precolonial cultural tradition. In other words, theoretical reflections suffer from significant ethnocentrism: the majority of researchers, paying scant attention to the history of the discipline, the former indigenous communities, or colonialism, tell us how the past truly was. In studying the past, archaeologists study "others" through the contemporary lens of their own time. Thus, there has been a sense of "othering" in archaeological research, based on a quest for knowledge and understanding of those distanced in time from the present.

Through the process of colonization, as Atalay (2006) has pointed out, Westerners acquired the power to study not only those who were distant from them in time, but also the past of others who were culturally, and often geographically, distant from them and who had been subjected to colonial rule around the globe. In these colonial contexts, the "othering" by archaeologists not only entails a distance in time but also a distance based on another, more cultural dimension: it has created a power imbalance that has allowed archaeologists to study the past ways of life of those who are not their own ancestors. Archaeologists have used Western epistemologies to view the practices and ways of life of others, many of whom held very different world views that operated through a different set of ontological and epistemological principles. Moreover this research, carried out for the benefit of Western scholars, was (re)produced using Western methods of recording history (external to people and contained in books, intended for purchase), and was taught in higher education institutions or sold to public audiences. However, the truth is that there should be a different approach: there is a particular need to deconstruct archaeology as a discipline. A decolonizing archaeology must include topics such as the social construction of cultural heritage, concerns over revitalizing tradition and the indigenous legacy, and the history and role of museums, collections, and collecting. We must ask questions about what it means to have one's history, story, or knowledge examined, interpreted, and displayed by "outsiders," and about who has access to this knowledge.

Defining the Canarian indigenous past on the basis of the culture concept, within the context of a nondecolonized archaeology, has invoked an inventory of cultural, linguistic, and material traits. The resulting picture has therefore been that of an indigenous people with a "museum culture," uprooted from the deep historical field and devoid of dynamism and meaning. The consequences of such an approach are not restricted to academic studies and reports but, as already stated, are also manifest in areas such as political policy, administrative practice, legislation, and heritage management. In this sense, the preservation of the indigenous Canarian heritage provides a typical example of this objectification of culture, whereby a body of static cultural characteristics becomes reified as an object possessed by the nation. The definition, inventory, and circumscribing of what is regarded as "authentic" indigenous culture is therefore embedded in a Western or globalized worldview. In the Canary Islands it seems that there is no way of moving forwards by engaging with a range of "other" concepts of history, culture, heritage, and the past in order to produce new ideas and new directions. There are no alternative interpretations of the archaeological record.

This scenario appears even bleaker if we observe the actual theoretical development of archaeology in Spain and, by extension, in the Canary Islands, where only small "islands" of debate and imported debate exist, empiricism and ingenuous positivism are more than hegemonic, and it may be said that, in many ways, we are facing a situation of "theoretical sclerosis" and chronic lack of debate. In Spain cultural historicism still prevails and this phenomenon brings with it, among other things, a lack of theoretical, conceptual, and interpretative debate, supplemented in many cases by nominalist discussions on typologies or methodology that have little or nothing to do with the historical–social problematics that enable us to interpret past societies in order to learn a little more about present-day societies. Within this scenario, the colonial discourse of Canarian archaeology does not contribute to the recovery of the Amazigh past of the islands. Also, the politics of the nondecolonized Canarian archaeology can hardly coexist with the Maghreb's evolution after the so-called "Arab spring," with the Berber/Amazigh culture movement, and with Canarian demands of independence from Spain, which are postulated appealing to Amazigh roots.

The great challenge, therefore, is to produce an archaeology that is not simply dedicated to importing theoretical models. Importing the latest theory (whether from Cambridge or Buenos Aires) is a step forward, but the next step must be to submit theoretical paradigms to critical scrutiny and propose new ways of looking at things. Naturally this does not mean that we must all believe that the new paradigms will be radically different from the existing ones. On the contrary, it is an important theoretical exercise to transform hegemonic approaches through detailed case studies using the methodological and theoretical tools at our disposal, through views based on local (political and scientific) experience in dialogue with the dominant Anglo-Saxon paradigms. In other words, theoretical archaeology implies dual reflection: first we must look outwards (not only in geographical terms, but also outside the discipline itself) and this reflection must then be turned on ourselves and be reflected in our practice. The reality of Canarian geography, namely its insularity, is not necessarily a problem: on the contrary, it can become a creative stimulus.

Finally, Canarian geography is characterized by very small areas of land and great expanses of ocean. It would be appropriate for future thematic studies in the region to focus deeply on the ways in which Canarian society and its archaeological heritage reflect the constraints and opportunities afforded by this environment.

References

Atalay, S. (2006). Indigenous archaeology as decolonizing practice. American Indian Quarterly, Vol. 30, No. 3/4, Special Issue: Decolonizing Archaeology (Summer—Autumn), pp. 280–310

Castillo, A. (Ed.). (2012). *Actas del Primer Congreso Internacional de Buenas Prácticas en Patrimonio Mundial: Arqueología*. Menorca, 9–13 de abril de 2012 (pp. 247–259). Madrid: Editora Complutense. https://portal.ucm.es/web/publicaciones/congresos. Accessed 13 Jan 2013

Farrujia, de la Rosa A. J. (2012). ¿Patrimonio Arqueológico, Patrimonio Mundial? En busca de la cultura Guanche en Aguere. In A. Castillo (Ed.), *Actas del Primer Congreso Internacional de Buenas Prácticas en Patrimonio Mundial: Arqueología*. Menorca, 9–13 de abril de 2012, (pp. 247–259). Madrid: Editora Complutense. https://portal.ucm.es/web/publicaciones/congresos. Accessed 11 Jan 2013

ICOMOS. (2005). *The world heritage list: Filling the gaps. An action plan for the future*. Paris: ICOMOS.

Ireland, T. (2002). Giving value to the Australian historic past: Archaeology, heritage and nationalism. *Australasian Historical Archaeology, 20*, 15–25.

Ireland, T. (2010). Excavating globalization from the ruins of colonialism: Archaeological heritage management responses to cultural change. ICOMOS Scientific Symposium changing world, changing views of heritage: The impact of global change on cultural heritage. http://www.international.icomos.org/adcom/dublin2010/Paper_2.pdf. Accessed 15 Jan 2013

Smith, L. (2006). *Uses of heritage*. London: Routledge.

Willems, J. H. W. (2012). World heritage and global heritage: The tip of the iceberg. In A. Castillo (Ed.), *Actas del Primer Congreso Internacional de Buenas Prácticas en Patrimonio Mundial: Arqueología. Menorca, 9–13 de abril de 2012*, (pp. 36–50). Madrid: Editora Complutense. https://portal.ucm.es/web/publicaciones/congresos. Accessed 29 Jan 2013

Index

A. J. Farrujia de la Rosa, *An archaeology of the margins,*
SpringerBriefs in Archaeology, DOI 10.1007/978-1-4614-9396-9,
© The Author(s) 2014

Printed by Printforce, the Netherlands